Alan   Campbell

from

Dick   Faber

March   2000

A CHAIN OF CITIES

' ... cities of men
And manners, climates, councils, governments,
... I am a part of all that I have met.'

(from Tennyson's *Ulysses*)

A CHAIN OF CITIES

Diplomacy at the End of Empire

Richard Faber

The Radcliffe Press
London · New York

Published in 2000 by The Radcliffe Press
Victoria House, Bloomsbury Square
London WC1B 4DZ
175 Fifth Avenue, New York NY 10010

In the United States and Canada
distributed by St Martin's Press
175 Fifth Avenue, New York NY 10010

ISBN 1–86064–594–1

A full CIP record for this book is available from the British Library
A full CIP record for this book is available from the Library of Congress

Library of Congress Catalog card: available

Typeset in Sabon by Oxford Publishing Services, Oxford
Printed and bound in Great Britain by WBC Ltd, Bridgend

Contents

Illustrations

Acronyms and Abbreviations

ACDA	Arms Control and Disarmament Agency
ADC	aide-de-camp
CCTA	Commission for Technical Cooperation in Africa
CIA	Central Intelligence Agency
DDT	dichlorodiphenyltrichloreoethane (insecticide)
FAMA	Foundation for Mutual Assistance in Africa
FCO	Foreign and Commonwealth Office
KGB	Komitet Gosudarstvennoi Bezopasnosti (Committee of State Security)
LCT	Landing Craft (Tank)
LST	Landing Ship (Tank)
MECAS	Middle East Centre for Arab Studies
MFH	Master of Foxhounds
MLF	multilateral force
NASA	National Aeronautics and Space Administration
NATO	North Atlantic Treaty Organization
OAS	Organisation Armée Secrète
NIBMAR	no independence before majority (African) rule
OUCA	Oxford University Conservative Association
OUDS	Oxford University Dramatic Society
RAF	Royal Air Force
RN	Royal Navy
RNR	Royal Naval Reserve
RNVR	Royal Navy Volunteer Reserve
TUC	Trades Union Congress
UDI	unilateral declaration of independence
UNESCO	United Nations Educational, Scientific, and Cultural Organization

1

Prospect

It was August 1949. Two Oxford friends and I were sitting in Constitution Square, in Athens, drinking something Greek and affordable. Dusk was beginning to gather. Having had a classical education I recalled vaguely that Pindar and Aristophanes had hailed Athens as being 'violet-crowned'. I fancied that this was the light that still hung over the city.

We did not think of ourselves as being tourists — though that is of course what we were. We were certainly not mass tourists, because foreign tourists in Greece, of any kind, were still rare birds. A few days before our arrival, bandits had held up a party of French archaeologists on the road to Delphi. When we got to Delphi ourselves we were at first alone in the hotel. The lavatories did not flush and almost the only food available was goat's meat or omelettes at a neighbouring café (our stomachs never recovered). Similarly, we were splendidly alone at Olympia, the Theatre of Epidauros and the field of Marathon. In Athens itself we were not quite alone when we saw the Acropolis; but there were no crowds or queues. Nico Henderson (newly arrived at the embassy) primed us with Athenian brandy, introduced us to a Greek academic lawyer and took us to see the ruins by moonlight.

There was a sprinkling of British soldiers and officers around in Constitution Square that evening; Britain was still expected to play a part in Greek affairs. But this influence

1

was waning rather than waxing. The Americans were more active, more numerous and had more to offer. American troops could be seen in the square as well as British, together with a still larger number of civilian members of the Marshall Aid mission. Wherever we travelled in Greece, signs on the cottages publicized an indisputable American achievement: spraying by DDT had removed the need for Keating's powder.

My two friends and I began to talk about careers. I had already taken my degree; but I was going back to Oxford for a term, because I had been elected President of the Union. After that I would join my father's publishing business unless I took some steps to do something else. My father, who was ambitious for me, would have liked me to become a publisher and then go into politics, as he had always wanted to do himself. I was quite ambitious, too. But I thought I would need more money to be a Conservative politician than I was ever likely to have. In any case I had reasonable doubts about whether I was thick-skinned enough.

It seemed probable that I would become a publisher, for the negative reason that there was nothing else I was particularly well fitted to do. I realized that I was lucky to have the chance of such an attractive job; but I did not want to have the choice of my career determined so effortlessly, or to find myself treading — less firmly than him — in my father's footsteps.

The Foreign Service (as it was then called) enjoyed quite a lot of prestige among my Oxford contemporaries, partly because the selection process was supposed to be rigorous. There were jokes about the need to have good table manners; but everybody knew that it was no longer necessary to have private means or foreign languages. As a boy scout at school, I had once dipped into a handbook on careers that listed the qualities required for diplomacy. I thought I had some of these, if not others. (Looking back, I think it was less a question of what qualities I had, than of what qualities I would like to have had.) More to the point, perhaps, my friends and I had been exposed in Athens to the charm and interest of life abroad. What we had seen of the British embassy had both impressed and amused us — but at least it had been intriguing. Without saying so, I decided that evening that, when I got home, I would find out whether I was too old to sit the Foreign Service entrance examination. Of course, I thought to myself, this commits me to nothing. But, as it turned out, I had committed myself for the best part of my life.

Because I had served three years in the navy, I was nearly 25. On my return I found I was only just eligible to apply. But apply I did. I got a sensationally low mark in a mathematical intelligence test. I might have scuppered my chances by being a bit too frank with an interviewing psychologist, or by telling the board (which included a TUC representative) that I had a particular horror of demagogy. I showed a dismal lack of historical ingenuity in an interview with a man from the Foreign Office. Nevertheless I passed in, respectably if not with flying colours. In August 1950, after some months in the Russell Square offices of Faber & Faber, I was working in the Northern Department of the Foreign Office.

* * *

Athens has meant much less to me than most of the other cities visited in this book. I have been back there three times, but never for more than a few hours. Yet it was the first, determining, link in the chain that patterned my working life.

These pages are an attempt to recapture that life and the upbringing behind it. It is a personal, rather than a diplo-

3

matic, memoir. I never kept diaries and have not consulted official documents. But I hope that what I have written, however impressionistic, is honest and accurate, so far as it goes.

I find it difficult to write much about former colleagues, whether alive or recently dead — most of them were friends as well. So there is too much about myself. I have no excuse, except that my own reactions are what I knew best at the time and remember best now.

* * *

I am grateful to a number of people for advice and encouragement in writing this book, particularly to my brother and sister-in-law, to my friend Philip Ziegler and to my colleague in Algiers, Brian Hitch.

2

Home

I was born on 6 December 1924 in a nursing home in Lexham Gardens. I believe it was a Saturday. My mother could never remember the exact moment of my arrival, though she thought it was around 9.00 p.m. This would have been a serious handicap if I had been born in China and needed a Chinese horoscope. A few years ago I was given a book on Chinese astrology; it was clear that precision was essential. There is a theory that one is at one's best — or at least at one's most cheerful — around the hour of one's birth. That would be no help in fixing the time. A lot of people feel cheerful at 9.00 p.m. on a Saturday night.

What my mother did probably remember, but never told me, was that I had to be pulled out feet first. I only heard about this quite recently from one of my nieces (a midwife); it is recorded in a diary kept by my father. Apparently I emerged from an hour-long ordeal hideous and quite bald — though I was later to grow a crop of bright red, curly hair. It seems to me a tribute to all concerned that, after this unorthodox start, I should have had a more or less normal life.

My father registered my birth a month later in the sub-district of South Kensington. He described himself as a barrister at law, living in 21 Ladbroke Grove. When my sister was born he had been a director of a family brewing business in Hampshire. By the time of my brother's birth he was running the publishing firm that began as Faber &

Gwyer and grew into Faber & Faber. In December 1924 he was negotiating his future career, but had no full-time occupation; he was called to the Bar, but never practised.

I cannot picture the house in Ladbroke Grove, though I have a dim memory of a dark staircase. When I was still quite small we moved to Oak Hill Park, a private road near Hampstead Heath. It had won a prize of some kind at the Great Exhibition of 1851; the houses were of that period, white and sedately Italianate. We lived first in number 7 and later in number 1. Nowadays, number 1 is the only Victorian villa that survives in the road and each of its four floors is a flat.

My father, at least before the war, would not have considered himself a wealthy man. When I asked my mother if we were rich, she firmly denied it (I expect she would have done so even if we had been), though she added that we were quite comfortably off. I was disappointed by this unexciting answer and tried again with social class. One of my mother's sisters said, rather deprecatingly, that we were a good middle-class family; under pressure she admitted: 'Well, perhaps upper-middle class.' I had to be content with that.

My father's ancestors had been yeoman sheep farmers in the West Riding of Yorkshire in the sixteenth and seventeenth centuries. In the eighteenth century one of them became a currier in Leeds and made enough money to have his two sons well educated. The elder qualified as a doctor, the younger (my ancestor) as an Anglican clergyman. Two generations later my great-grandfather, also in orders, was a don at Oxford at the time of the Oxford movement; one of his brothers, Father Faber, followed Newman to Rome, wrote well-known hymns and became the first superior of the Brompton Oratory. My grandfather, whom I never knew, was a housemaster at Malvern College. Meanwhile, another branch of the family, no longer flourishing, had risen in the world; of four Edwardian brothers two were ennobled, as Lords Faber and Wittenham, while a third became a fox-hunting MP and a fourth bought the Hampshire brewery where my father began his married life.

My mother's surname was Richards; the family were anglicized Welsh from the neighbourhood of Dolgelly. Her father, an international lawyer, served for a time on the council of the viceroy of India and later became Chichele Professor of International Law at Oxford. My grandmother, who was rather beautiful, had nine brothers (one of them fathered Rab Butler); my grandfather told his prospective father-in-law jauntily that he had come 'to take Isabel off the shelf'; she had had to take refuge in the lavatory to read his love letters in peace. My grandfather's ancestor, a farmer's son, had a distinguished legal career in the early nineteenth century, becoming Sir Richard Richards or 'Double Dick' to his friends; he married into the local gentry and retired to a big house on the outskirts of Dolgelly, which is still standing.

Thus, on both sides of the family, the provenance was typical enough of the established professional class before the war: clergymen, lawyers and a few soldiers in the nineteenth century; yeoman farmers, minor gentry and farm labourers in earlier periods. The overall picture is not very different from the account of his ancestors given by Evelyn Waugh in his autobiography.

Middle-class life before the war was of course in many ways unlike what it is now. We lived, on the whole, in larger houses; they were usually colder (though there was always one warm room); meals were more regular and often more substantial. We had cooked breakfasts; lunch was two courses; in the evenings my parents ate soup, a main dish with vegetables and a savoury. During my childhood we always had a cook, a housemaid and a parlour maid; when we were small there was also a nanny or a children's maid

— at one time both. This was not, then, at all out of the way; grander households had butlers and three-course lunches. It was only when the war came that my mother learned how to cook and my brother and I had to wash up.

We saw much less of our parents than children do nowadays. For one thing, when we were small, we had separate meals in the nursery. For another, we were tucked up in bed before my father came home from work. He gave us some time on Sundays; but I do not remember him telling us stories, or helping us with our homework. I only recall being hugged by him on one occasion, when I had been unhappy at school and my mother urged him to come home early to console me. I took all this as normal and never felt in any way starved of love. I did, however, find it difficult to confide in my father until I was a good deal older.

My mother was not a great hugger either. But she loved children and I believe would have been glad to spend much of the day with us. She did not do so, because it was not the custom and she did not like to get in the nanny's way. We were taken down to her at about teatime, when she would play with, or read to, us. On one evening a week and every other Sunday the nanny had time off; then to my great delight, my mother would take charge.

This does not imply that we had much to suffer from any of our nannies. One of them, a young Scotswoman called Cathy, tried to make us eat the oily underskin of kippers. She would also come and look at us before she went to bed; this was only right and proper, but she made it too obvious that she did not like to find us awake. As a result I could never fall asleep before she came. I screwed myself up for her arrival, simulating sleep as well as I knew how. She would peer at me suspiciously, but would eventually leave me in peace. Then, rapidly and invariably, I dropped off.

I can remember being put into gaiters for walks on the heath. In the mornings I woke up to the sounds of horse-drawn milk carts; the United Dairy's cart was red, the Express Dairy's cart was blue; I never decided which I liked best. When it came to the boat race, however, there was no room for doubt; out of family piety we passionately supported the dark blues. Our nannies preferred the lighter colour and we had to make the best of a series of Oxford defeats. On one occasion I ran downstairs to my mother, chanting happily: 'Nanny's won the boat race. But we've won the toss! We've won the toss!'

I was not very fond of one of Cathy's predecessors, who had a moustache. She was not very fond of me either, perhaps because I called her 'Nanny Blinky' from the way she swivelled her eyes. One day my father was at home and took me to the Whitestone Pond. I liked it and fell in; he had to fish me out with his walking stick and bear me, dripping, home. Nanny Blinky, about to go out, was not pleased to see me. 'Drat the child,' she said unpleasantly, perhaps forgetting that my father was there. He thought this was not the right spirit and made my mother sack her.

Amateur psychology was becoming fashionable in the late 1920s. Some years later my parents admitted to me that I had begun to whine a good deal; even before my immersion, they had feared that Nanny Blinky was not doing me much good. I shall never know what I would have been like without her. Perhaps I would have had more self-confidence — but perhaps I would have had too much of it.

I learned to read at home, from Victorian primers, which I think must have taught my mother when she was a girl. At the age of five I went to a kindergarten in Hampstead run by two ladies, one stout and the other slim; my parents thought I owed a good deal to a younger teacher whom we all adored. Then, when I was about eight, I went for three years to a preparatory day school on the Finchley Road. My time there is quite clear in my memory, but I do not know that it had very much bearing on my future life. I wrote (for my own satisfaction) quite a bit of historical verse, full of rhymes and rhythm; I still treasure a moving lament about the parting of Prince Charlie and Flora Macdonald. I discovered that I had a good voice and enjoyed singing. I was pushed into an inconclusive fight with another boy on the asphalt playground; I had no trust in my fighting ability and was relieved — though my opponent was disgusted — when, after a short exchange of blows, the result was proclaimed a draw. I must, of course, have learned various things, like the names of Norfolk towns and the dates of our kings and queens: as a potential scholarship boy I was introduced to the Greek alphabet before I left the school. But most of what I now know I learned later.

In 1930 my parents bought a house in Cardiganshire, four miles from the coast, together with 63 acres of land. It was quite a large house, though the rooms were not particularly spacious, and it was then about a hundred years old. I would have liked it to be older and was sorry that there were no secret passages; but it counted locally as a 'mansion' because it had two staircases. There was a lovely view at the back of the house, bounded by hills; to the right was the River Aeron, to the left an avenue of trees known as the Beech Walk. In the spring the sloping field below the house was yellow with daffodils.

For the next ten years or so we spent all our school holidays there. My father sometimes had to go up to London; but he was his own master and could do as he liked. Whenever he was at home, throughout my childhood and adolescence, he retired to his study in the forenoons and between tea and dinner in the late afternoons. I suppose he kept in touch with the firm by correspondence. In the afternoons he would do some rough shooting (mostly rabbits) or — in the summer — take us for picnics on neighbouring beaches.

From the age of ten I was at boarding schools; so Tyglyn

Aeron became my home, rather than the house in Hampstead. As I look back it seems to me that the three of us had an unusual, and very privileged, childhood. It was not luxurious and we were expected to entertain ourselves. We were given very little pocket money and were seldom taken to cinemas. But we had 63 acres at our disposal; we had a swimming pool and a tennis court; we even had a kind of stage on which we acted in grease paint and cast-off clothes. There were interesting grown-up guests from time to time, notably T. S. Eliot, my brother's godfather, who always came equipped with expensive presents and practical jokes. In one of my sister's last stage productions — before she got too old for them — I spouted several lines from *Dr Faustus* to an audience consisting of him and my mother. I remember feeling in a sort of trance, completely carried outside myself. Afterwards Uncle Tom (which was what we called him) had a volume of Marlowe's plays sent to me, so I suppose he thought that I should be encouraged.

Above all, the house was always overflowing with books since, besides bought or inherited volumes, parcels of the firm's latest productions kept on arriving. I read voraciously, mostly novels and histories, both new and old. Of course, there was no television and there was not much listening to the wireless before the years of the *Brains Trust* and Priestley's wartime broadcasts. On the other hand, there was a magnificent gramophone with a horn, together with a large collection of 78 records. We heard a lot of classical music, as well as comic records (*Double Damask* and *A Cure for Hiccoughs* by Cicely Courtneidge seemed to me hysterically funny). In the evenings we took it in turns reading aloud from Dickens, Trollope, or Jane Austen. We all liked showing off in this way; so my father had to be strict in rationing the time — until he came to his own turn.

My parents got to know most of the local gentry. There were children's parties, particularly at Christmas time, in one or two of the larger houses. There was also a pack of beagles kennelled near one of them. The theory was that the hare ran round in circles, enabling the grown-ups to sit on shooting sticks in the middle, while the children staggered round the circumference with the hunt staff. To be honest, it was more of a penance than a pleasure. But we went home to mustard baths and baked beans.

The 1930s began in economic depression and ended in war. On the whole it was not a very satisfactory decade. Later, as I grew up, I thought that there had been too much hollowness in those years, not enough acceptance of reality. The old social structure survived, but the rich felt increasingly guilty. We were still proud of our empire, but reluctant to face sacrifices for it. The Englishman's home was his castle, but it was often a small mock-Tudor house in a ribbon development. American cultural imports, from snappy slang to swing music and animated cartoons, began to swamp our own creations. However, between the depression and the war, there was a period of relative hope and prosperity, when some people managed to feel progressive and be conservative at the same time. Faber & Faber publications circulated round London in a yellow vehicle flaunting the legend: 'Faber Books are in the Van.' In Wales we felt quite modern as we drove to the seaside in brightly coloured Aertex shirts, or sipped sundaes in an Aberystwyth milk bar.

There was one drawback to the way of life in our 'demi-paradise'. We (or at least I) never felt that we really belonged to Cardiganshire. We could not speak Welsh, though we sometimes tried feebly to learn it. We had few friends of our own age, except those who came to stay. People were kind to us and my mother's Welsh origins helped. But we were seen as rich English people using the house as a holiday home. I do not think there was much nationalist resentment then in our area — after all, we gave

12

occasional employment and bought local supplies. Nevertheless, we were exotic and detached. There was no real attempt, either by the village children or by us, to get to know each other.

I think this had some lasting consequences for me. Even in London I never felt that I fully belonged, because Lexham Gardens must have been well beyond the sound of Bow bells; besides, for several of my formative years, I spent more time in the country than there. Yet there was no country district with which I could identify. To this day I do not know what to say when asked by people where I come from. I have never felt part of any regional community; even if I wanted to, I cannot imagine what football team I would support. Whether, subconsciously, this motivated my choice of career, or whether my career simply confirmed me in an existing disposition, I could not say. With my feeling for the past I wanted roots; I could find them in my family, but not in any one place.

We were in Cardiganshire when war broke out. I remember hearing Chamberlain talk about 'evil things' on the radio. My father was annoyed with me because, in a fit of escapism, I wanted to read about Marie Antoinette rather than to listen to the latest bulletins. The first night, however, I went to bed firmly expecting something very exciting to happen before dawn. Nothing, of course, did. Next day we went to a big house to stuff pillows for evacuees. The gardener's boy joined up. Otherwise, for a time, life went on as before.

In 1941 my father sold the house. It had become too difficult to keep it going, and to move between it and London, in wartime. We spent one or two holidays in the Hampstead house, where the garage had been converted into a sandbagged air-raid shelter. Then its lease expired. In 1942 my parents moved to a comfortable Edwardian house called Minsted, near Midhurst in West Sussex. My father had bought it for All Souls College (having been their estates bursar in his spare time for years) together with over 600 acres of fields and woods. He rented the house from the college; later he had to buy a herd of Ayrshires from them and rent the fields as well. Minsted was my only home for a couple of years before I joined the navy and for another three years when I was at the university. Afterwards I visited it quite often at weekends until my father's death in 1961. I associate it with many experiences, most of them pleasant; but it never had the place in my imagination that Tyglyn Aeron had had.

3
Education

School (1935–43)

Boys who went to preparatory boarding schools usually did so around the age of eight. I was nearly eleven when I arrived at the Dragon School in North Oxford. I cannot remember how I got there (I suppose by the 4.45 train from Paddington), but my first impressions of the place are among my most vivid memories. Although apprehensive, I had been cautiously optimistic. My parents had visited the school and my mother had painted an idealized picture of its peaceful and civilized atmosphere. As soon as I entered the door of School House I realized that it was not going to be like that. Clutching my hand luggage I stood forlornly by the staircase, with boys who already knew the building milling and shrieking around. At that moment the headmaster's son came downstairs and somehow identified me. 'Ah, Richard,' he said to me unctuously, rubbing his hands; then he put a boy in charge of me.

Later I got to like Joc Lynam, who had a dynamic charm and was a very effective organizer and disciplinarian. But I was not used to his rather histrionic manner, which struck me as frighteningly hypocritical. Having read some Dickens, I immediately felt that I had arrived at Dotheboys Hall, or its equivalent.

Of course the Dragon School had little or nothing in common with Dotheboys Hall. But I did suffer a good deal during my first year there. This was not so much because I was homesick or because I was badly bullied. It was more that I did not want to do the things that the boys in my group seemed to want to do. That might not have mattered if, at the same time, I had not very much wanted to be liked.

When my parents became aware that I was unhappy, my father wrote to the headmaster suggesting that I should be moved to a different dormitory, but imploring him not to say anything either to me or to the other boys. Hum Lynam believed that, if you appealed to their better instincts, boys could be gentlemen. Up to a point — though only up to a point — he may have been right. After he had spoken to them (without my knowledge) the other boys probably did soften their behaviour a little; next term I was moved to another, rather more congenial, dormitory. It was only a few months later that I learned what had happened, when I found myself back in another dormitory with some of the old gang. It seemed to me then that nothing worse could have happened to me and that I had been branded for life. I realized that both my father and the headmaster had tried to act for the best; but that could not remove my sense of having been betrayed.

Even at the time, still more later, I used to think that this and other experiences had toughened me up and made me fitter for a life of action. Sometimes, nowadays, I wonder whether my imagination might have flourished better in a less bracing environment. I do not know the answer. I suspect, however, that, if I had been differently educated, I would not have ended up in the government service.

I survived and, by the end of my time at the school, had a normal quota of friends. This was in spite of my incompetence at games, which played a very important part in the eyes of most of the boys and many of the masters. I found rugger disagreeable and cricket boring — and both of them pointless. (If I had been naturally good at them, it would have been a different story.) For half of one term I came into my own, because I was quite good at athletics. Otherwise, I had to depend on other talents — singing and acting ability — for any prestige. The school was very good at encouraging such talents, as well as sports. A Gilbert and Sullivan operetta was performed every December, a Shakespeare play every February. I was Grosvenor in *Patience* and Marco in *The Gondoliers*. My performance as Lady Macbeth, in a black wig, was admired more than anything I have done in later life. I played it absolutely straight, as children do, without any theories or any suggestion of sex. I suppose the effect was single-minded — and, after all, that is what Lady Macbeth was.

I shared a tiny garden with another boy. I also spent a good deal of time in the art school, creating brightly-coloured historical and mythical scenes in poster paints. My best friend, James Tranchell, told me that the art mistress, a rather unadventurous, middle-aged lady, gave me prizes because she was afraid of me. He said that the clue to my personality was fear. This would have flattered me if I could have believed it; but I think he must have been reading a magazine article on psychology. James (actually we called each other by our surnames) was a clever and precocious boy, who would have regarded himself as a failure in life without a scholarship to Winchester. He did get one; but, before he could take it up and just after I had moved on to Westminster, he was killed in a traffic accident.

In the summer holidays we were urged to keep diaries, which were read and marked by the 'Skipper', Hum Lynam's elder brother, who had founded the school. I put quite a lot into mine and got a good mark. The Skipper wrote kindly on the flyleaf: 'Capital descriptive powers — I am sure he will be a writer one day.' At least I am still trying.

The teaching at the school was good, though more

efficient than inspired. I was too slapdash mentally to be an accurate scholar; so I had to be drilled. The emphasis was on Latin and Greek, which won scholarships; I particularly remember slogging through Greek irregular verbs and being trained to tackle unseen translations. My English poetic taste was formed, almost exclusively, on Tennyson. Later it broadened a bit; but (with the exception of T. S. Eliot) I have never found it easy to relish modern poets. I went on writing conventional verse myself until I was about 40; then the wells of occasional inspiration dried up.

International tensions made themselves felt from time to time. I would now class the Lynams as socially progressive Conservatives. Joc was a great fan of Edward VIII. Another master justified Italian actions in Abyssinia; on one occasion German schoolboys treated us to a concert as part of a Nazi charm offensive. But I think we were more influenced by what we heard of foreign affairs at home. I did not hear very much until a year or so before the war. At the beginning of one term a friend asked me which side I was on in the Spanish Civil War. He darted the question at me, expecting an immediate answer. I had no idea. I think I said 'Loyalist', because that sounded good. One of the younger masters made the members of his class act as special correspondents in each of the European capitals. We had to read the newspapers and report briefly to the class each morning on current events in our chosen countries. I had picked Paris, which must already have had some special interest for me.

My last term was largely given up to scholarship hunting. My parents had agreed with my teachers that I should try for Eton; if that failed, I should go for Westminster, which had its scholarship examination (called the 'Challenge') later in the summer. Together with a few other boys I went to Windsor and stayed (for almost the first time in my life) at a hotel. This was exciting and the atmosphere of the school, in golden sunshine, was seductive. But my papers, particularly in Latin and Greek, were not good enough. I ought to have done better in the English essay. However, I elected to fulminate against the *Daily Mirror* for its handling of the abdication crisis. These were my sincere views and would still be today; but I suspect that the examiners thought I was retailing the sentiments of a blimpish relative. I must have been overexcited throughout the examination, because I kept on wanting to go to the lavatory. Each time I had to ask permission from a hawk-nosed invigilator, each time he looked at me as if I had a crib concealed somewhere in the panelling.

By the time of the Challenge we were (I think) in quarantine; so I was allowed to take the papers peacefully at the Dragon School. Shortly before the results were published my mother had to take me for an interview with the Head Master at his house in Dean's Yard. When we left, Mr Christie said something about hoping to see me again. My mother immediately realized that I had won a scholarship; she did not tell me so and I had to wait a few more hours until we got a telegram. To pass the time we took a bus to Swiss Cottage to see a Fred Astaire film. When I went to bed the telegram had arrived and I felt like a hero.

I cannot remember going into College at Westminster for the first time; but my first impressions must have been quite different from my abandonment of hope on the threshold of School House. I think I knew, almost immediately, that I was going to like the place. For one thing, the buildings and traditions were steeped in the antiquity that always attracted me. For another, I boarded with other scholarship boys and could talk to them about the things that I found interesting. Like Eton and Winchester, Westminster is an old foundation, having a special house, known as 'College', for scholarship holders. We were called 'King's Scholars' and wore short gowns on top of our black morning coats or Eton jackets. We had to get used to people looking at us in the streets. An old man once growled 'Sybarite' at me. I suppose he looked on me as a spoilt sprig of the aristocracy; I felt anything but sybaritic in my stiff collar and heavy clothes.

I had a cubicle ('house') to myself in the scholars' dormitory, which Lord Burlington was thought to have designed. My house was almost alone in having a sash window that opened onto Little Dean's Yard. I was very proud of this, though it meant that anything not kept in a drawer got covered with soot. My most intense moments there occurred during a religious phase, when I prepared myself for early Communion with the aid of a devotional manual given to me by my Faber grandmother. A less edifying memory is of my using Dr Page-Barker's Scurf Lotion — an unpleasantly sticky and smelly fluid — to try to make my hair straighter.

The food at the Dragon School had been healthful but uninviting. The only menu I really enjoyed there was the boiled egg served to each of us — together with a fresh orange — for Sunday breakfast. Once a year we were instructed to cheer the cook when she made a special effort and produced pancakes on Shrove Tuesday. She also specialized in a particularly nasty soup, sometimes leaving her hairpins in it. Joc Lynam would come into the dining room with a bowl of this, licking his lips and exclaiming, in his theatrical way: 'Delicious School House soup! Quite delicious!' But he never took us in. At Westminster, on the other hand, the food was good. We ate it in College Hall, just by the Abbey, on tables supposed to have been made out of the wrecked timbers of the Spanish Armada.

My religious phase was brought on by my Confirmation. It did not last very long, at least in its pristine intensity. The following year I read George Moore's *The Brook Kerith* and began to think that, after all, perhaps Jesus was not the Son of God in a unique sense. Later I wondered what I meant by

God and whether I had any proofs of His existence. Above all I was puzzled by the knowledge that some people, whom I respected, said they believed in God and others, whom I respected equally, said they did not. I remarked on this once to my housemaster, who was temperately devout. It did not seem to worry him at all. But I still find it difficult to believe that any particular group of fallible human beings holds the key to existence. Agnostics cannot claim to hold it either — but then they explicitly profess ignorance. At Westminster I was in no hurry to proclaim myself either an atheist or an agnostic. I went on professing Christianity until my time at Oxford.

It was of course a pleasure for somebody with my historical and aesthetic tastes to take part in services in the Abbey. On Sundays those King's Scholars who had not gone home put on white surplices and figured in the procession of clergy and choristers. Beforehand, we lined the entrance, taking off our caps (mortarboards) to our elders and betters. Anybody wearing a top hat — there were not many at that time — was entitled to be 'capped'. In between services one could swim in an underground pool in Thames House, explore Westminster, or go to a gallery or museum.

I only had a year in the shadow of the Abbey. The war came and we were evacuated to Lancing College, where the religion was higher and the food plainer. When Lancing was taken over by the navy we moved again, for the second half of the summer term, to the University of the South-West at Exeter. I am glad to have seen that beautiful city before it was bombed. We boarded in a large mid-Victorian villa looking out over an Italianate garden. We rowed, not too energetically, on the placid river. The food was fully back to standard.

This was still 'the phoney war'; there had been little, if any, bombing. The governors decided that we could safely return to London in the autumn; Westminster had always been as much a day as a boarding school and numbers had fallen badly. It was only when all the preparations were complete — the last bed having been reportedly labelled — that the Blitz began. For two or three weeks some of us attended day classes at Westminster, equipped with our gas masks; sometimes we went on to the famous lunchtime concerts at the National Gallery; sometimes there were air-raid warnings. Then we moved to Herefordshire for the rest of the war.

In Herefordshire we occupied four or five large houses in the district around Bromyard. We shed our black clothes for shorts and open-neck shirts. College was housed in Whitbourne Court, belonging to the Harington family. It was full of atmosphere, which I relished, and haunted by a headless huntsman, whom I would have liked to meet. In the afternoons we cleared the attics, dug the flowerbeds and painted the woodwork; there was much less playing of games than there had been before evacuation. Later on we singled swedes and lifted potatoes for local farmers, who rewarded us with substantial cream teas, sometimes with small glasses of perry or cider. Three days a week we had to bicycle five or six miles, up and down hills and in all sorts of weather, to get to our lessons. It was quite strenuous, but a good way of seeing how the seasons changed the look of a lovely stretch of country.

The school had a first-class music master, Arnold Foster, who formed a good choir, including women from the village. A friend of mine in college produced *Richard II* — with me in the title role — in the village hall. The following year I produced *King Henry IV* (Part 2) in College Hall at Westminster, next door to the Jerusalem Chamber where Henry IV actually died. There was no attempt to keep up the Latin play, which College had produced annually in Lord Burlington's dormitory before the war.

The level of teaching obviously depended on the availability of masters in wartime. The Head Master, J. T. Christie, was the best teacher I have ever come across. He had a capacity to electrify, which I have never found in other schoolmasters. Another brilliant, rather subversive, teacher was the history master, John Bowle; but I did not have many lessons from him because, under the influence of the Head Master and my father, I specialized as a classical scholar. I had taken my school certificate in my first year at Westminster; after that we were obliged to choose between classics, history, modern languages, mathematics and science. Of course, we sometimes had lessons in subjects other than Latin and Greek. I remember gratefully a youngish English master, called Snelling, who encouraged me to believe that I could write.

In my last year I got my higher certificate and won a closed scholarship to Christ Church, Oxford. I was also appointed captain of college and head of the school. I had never thought of myself as a 'born leader' and can only assume that I was chosen because, in my year, there was nobody who really stood out. The Head Master preferred to have a King's Scholar as head of the school because, like Plato, he believed in 'philosopher kings'. I could act the part. But I am not sure that I was meant to be philosophically regal. I took the job seriously — too seriously. This was not very good for my character, though I suppose I muddled through.

I left Westminster before the summer term of 1943, in order to spend a few months at Oxford as part of a scheme designed to turn out RNVR officers. I looked on this as something of a soft option; it had been strongly pressed on my father by an RN captain whom he came across. It certainly enabled me to become an officer sooner, and more smoothly, than I could otherwise have expected to do.

People who disapproved of public schools used to criticize them on three main grounds: corporal punishment, homosexuality and 'the old school tie'. I have never had the loathing for corporal punishment that is now so often felt and expressed. Once or twice a master took a slipper to me at the Dragon School; once I was given four strokes of the cane by a monitor at Westminster. I was not conscious of any sadism and never felt the least resentment. As captain of college I had the second year boys 'tanned' on one occasion, for a collective breach of discipline; it had a noticeable, though of course not a permanent, effect. In doing this I was relying on the traditional powers of my predecessors; I knew that my housemaster was not in favour of corporal punishment; I would myself have been strongly against it, if it had been sadistic or excessive.

As regards homosexuality, naturally the older boys at Westminster, including myself, were apt to be attracted by the prettier young ones. There was suppressed desire and some attempts at romantic flirtation. I was myself never aware of it going any further than that. Perhaps it did; it had certainly done so at times in the past. But privacy was difficult to achieve and I can only record my own experience.

The old school tie, or the old boy network, was — perhaps still is — regarded as opening doors and procuring jobs undeservedly. Here again I can only write from my experience. My having been an old Westminster was never of the slightest advantage to me either in my work or in my personal dealings in later life. Perhaps it would have been more of an advantage to be an old Etonian; but, in the postwar government service, I am doubtful even of that. As far as I know, I only worked with two old Westminsters during my time in the Foreign/Diplomatic Service. One was my first ambassador, with whom I had very few dealings of any kind. The other was my predecessor as ambassador, who was never in any position to affect my career.

Having said this, I know I was lucky to have such a rich and enjoyable education as Westminster, even in wartime, provided. I have never doubted this. There was a slightly hothouse temperature in college after evacuation; it helped to bring to blossom whatever buds we had.

* * *

Afterwards (1943–50)

I had no naval connections and had never messed about in boats. I opted to go into the navy, rather than the army, because a friend of mine at Westminster gave me the idea and I did not think I would be good at hand-to-hand fighting. No doubt there were risks at sea; but they would presumably call for endurance rather than aggressive courage. In the event, I saw no action in the navy — and probably would not have seen any in the army, either. There were of course fewer young men sacrificed in the Second than in the First World War; the victims were mostly three or four years older than I was.

My few months at Oxford, in the summer of 1943, were largely a waste of time. I felt uncomfortable about this, when soldiers not much older than me, including my sister's fiancé, were being killed in North Africa. One or two days a week we wore bell-bottom trousers and learned to tie knots or send messages by Morse code and semaphore. Otherwise, I went to lectures and tutorials on Plato, Homer and Molière — none of them (except the last) breaking new ground. At the end of the course we moved on, as full-time naval cadets, to HMS *Ganges*, a training establishment near Ipswich; there I learned Scottish dancing, among other things, and for the first time heard four-letter words in regular use. After that we had a few weeks on the lower deck of a cruiser at Rosyth. It was bitterly cold and we had to holystone the decks in bare feet — something (I suspect) that only officer cadets could be made to do. There was a likeable RN lieutenant who tried to instil in us a feeling for the welfare of the ratings whom we would before long have to order about. Perhaps he succeeded, since I recall his words; they fitted in well enough with the notions I already had of how an officer was meant to behave.

I suppose one or two aspirants dropped out during this process. Otherwise we all turned up at Lancing College for the final stage of our transformation into officers. There was a good deal of parade ground drill. I got some quite undeserved prestige with the instructor by forcing my squad through an incorrect manoeuvre; working myself up I called them a 'bunch of cauliflowers'; the phrase was too picturesque, but I was thought to have displayed powers of command. We also got a grounding in seamanship, navigation and pilotage; in particular, if we were to be watch-keeping officers, we needed a thorough grasp of the rule of the road.

We moved from Lancing to Hove, then went to Greenwich for a fortnight's polish and the best food I had anywhere during the war. Some of us spent a farewell evening in a grand hotel, downing brandies and choking over cigars. (I suppose we had officer uniforms by then.) Then we awaited our appointments.

I served in three warships, as an RNVR midshipman and later as RNVR sub-lieutenant, before I was demobilized in the autumn of 1946. The first of these ships was HMS *Altair*, which had been the private yacht of a shipping magnate. It was not very large; but the wardroom had wooden panelling and my cabin was simple but comfortable. The yacht had been adapted to train officers in anti-submarine warfare. When I joined her she was being refitted at Glasgow and looked scruffy as well as tiny. Nobody seemed to be on deck, though eventually a still scruffier-looking rating appeared. Fresh from my training I had some of the hopeless feeling that had overwhelmed me at School

House. I got on all right with the other officers, but none of them was a soul mate; although I was rather a pet of the captain, a Welsh RNR (formerly Merchant Navy) officer who detested Freemasons, he usually kept to his cabin. Outside the wardroom I was continually worried about how far I should, or could, try to enforce correctness in such an incorrect atmosphere. I was right not to try too hard; but, at the time, I thought I was being cowardly.

When the refit was finished (including some French polishing of the wardroom, which the captain somehow wangled), we took up station at Campbeltown, on the Mull of Kintyre, and settled into a fixed routine. Each morning, fairly early, we cast off and went out to sea, together with that day's quota of trainees. Though I had nothing to do with submarine detection and its instruments, I kept watch on the bridge every forenoon. Then we had a greasy lunch of roast pork and plum duff in the wardroom. By that time the sea would always be rough and I always felt sick; retiring to my cabin I tried to read Gibbon's *Decline and Fall of the Roman Empire* in a small-print edition. I would emerge in time to help bring the ship back to port and to secure her alongside. In the evenings I sometimes met a friend from one of the other training yachts, for a beer or a rum in one of the quieter Campbeltown pubs. Once there was a party attended by a few officers as well as by ratings. A furious row developed between one of our petty officers (a former fisherman) and another man. I began to feel that I ought to do something about it. Luckily, a kindly older rating steered me out of trouble.

After six months of this it was time for a change. When the change came, however, it was an appointment to a boom defence vessel in Aden. This seemed to me so inglorious that I went up to the Admiralty and impersonated a keen young man of the right sort, eager for action. I was interviewed by a languid lieutenant commander, who was presumably reconciled to shore life. 'There aren't any destroyers available just now,' he said. 'There's an LST going to Australia.' Knowing nothing about landing ships, I hesitated. 'Nice ships,' he said in an offhand way. I realized that I would not get another chance — and took it.

I joined Landing Ship (Tank) 368 in Liverpool at the beginning of 1945. In the end we did not go to Australia, but to India, carrying an LCT and Royal Marines. The ship had been built in the USA for the Italian landings and was supposed to be expendable. However, she was still functioning, more or less, though her engines tended to break down from time to time. The Scottish engineer, who was almost permanently drunk, kept them going somehow — at any rate the captain (another RNR officer) had an immense faith in him, which I suppose must have been justified. Before we left England there was an additional, man-made cause of engine failure. A stoker, whose partner was pregnant, put some sand into the engines so that he could stay and look after her. We had a quiet man from Scotland Yard on board for a few days; it did not take him long to solve the mystery. I was officer of the day when the culprit was arrested and had to ensure that there was no sharp instrument within his reach. A court martial was held in HMS *Victory* at which I gave formal evidence in my most expensive, doeskin, uniform. To some people's indignation the sentence amounted to only two years' imprisonment, a comparatively lenient punishment, considering the gravity of such an offence in wartime.

Another thing I did before we left Portsmouth was to lay in a stock of bayonet fencing gear, as well as vaulting horses, mats and other aids to keeping fit. I was an assiduous reader of *Admiralty Fleet Orders* and had discovered that we were entitled to this equipment. Some of it was used, though not very often; the bayonet fencing gear was left to rust unseen.

Apart from keeping watches, my particular responsibilities in LST 368 were food, both for officers and for ratings, and recreation for the ship's company. Whenever we came into a port I would try to find a football team that could play our one; I would also, with the help of the supply petty officer, stock up on refrigerated carcasses and whatever fresh vegetables and fruit we could find. We got much of these in return for packets of cigarettes. Catering was full of pitfalls. Tripe for instance, was popular with the northcountrymen on board, but with nobody else.

We sailed out, through the Bay of Biscay and Suez Canal, to Cochin in India. There was plenty of rough weather, but no torpedoes or submarines. Afterwards, we moved from one Indian port to another, carrying various cargoes, from coal (on one occasion) to Indian troops. LSTs have long foredecks. From the bridge I could watch Sikhs sitting on their vehicles; they seemed to be endlessly occupied, like mermaids, in combing their uncut hair.

We took part in the liberation of Burma. The Japanese abandoned Rangoon, without our having to fight them; but it was still full of their condoms and cigarettes. Later we sailed with the big armada that landed on the Malayan coast. Again, there was no fighting. If there had been, we could have been in serious trouble because we were unable to get close enough inshore. At other times, we spent weeks in Trincomalee and in Singapore and sailed halfway up the river to Bangkok.

I had some leave in Darjeeling, visited the Shwedagon pagoda in Rangoon and saw quite a bit of the interior of Ceylon. So there were pleasures as well as chores. Brilliantly starlit skies relieved the gloomy middle watch; sometimes a scented offshore breeze would cheer the morning watch (a good watch anyway). The worst thing was not the heat, or any other discomfort, but the sense that most of the men were 'browned off', now that the war was effectively over, and wanted to get back to their families and girlfriends. One of the most disagreeable chores was censoring their letters to make sure that no enemy agent could discover where we were. The letters had been, almost invariably, 'Sealed with a Loving Kiss' (SWALK for short); but we had to unseal them.

In due course, we handed the ship back to the Americans. Then I came home in LST 3010, which was heavier and had been built in Britain. She was commanded by a young RN lieutenant commander; the other officers were, like me, RNVR: I was less anxious to be popular with the ship's company than I had been in LST 368. Starting in a new ship I thought I might find things easier if I kept my distance more and opened up less. In any case I was only going to serve in her for a few months. So I felt less involved and do not remember so much now. Watch-keeping apart, I did the sort of work that a paymaster would have done in a larger ship. I spent a good deal of time totting up figures, without a calculator, in a tiny office — one of the few parts of the ship, other than the wardroom, to have stayed in my mind.

The actual voyage home, too, is virtually a blank until we approached Italy. Then we anchored somewhere near Stromboli and bathed happily in the warm sea, before going on to Naples for a short stop. Together with two other young officers, I hired a taxi to Pompeii. Our Italian driver hurried us through the ruins, pausing only at any hint of a 'knocking shop'; then he took us to a café, where we sat outside, eating peaches and drinking local wine. We felt blissfully peaceful, but began to be worried by time, though our driver kept on reassuring us that there was no hurry. Eventually we forced him into the car and got back, just as the ship was lifting anchor, to find the captain in an understandably tense mood. 'You believe in cutting things fine, don't you?' he said. 'Yes, Sir' I said respectfully (I did not, but it seemed better not to argue). He snorted and turned on his heels. In a few days we would be beyond his control.

The voyage ended at Devonport. A friend of my sister's, who lived at Plymouth, had read of our homecoming in the local press, which had announced that friends and relatives would be welcome. Scarcely had we tied up alongside before I saw her and my mother waving at me. I am afraid it was more of a shock than a pleasure. No other friends or relatives had responded to the call. I had been away for the best part of two years and, on the voyage home as on the voyage out, had grown a straggly beard. I introduced my mother to the captain and others on board; they were polite, but we were none of us really ready for such a rapid return to normal life.

Next day, however, I was released and took a train, with my mother, to Sussex; in the otherwise empty compartment we slipped back, easily, into our old relationship. I only had a few days at home before the Oxford year began. There was time for my father to tell me that my beard made him feel old. Dutifully, I had it shaved off by a London barber. 'Smartening ourselves up a bit, are we Sir, now we're back in town?' he enquired amiably. My face stared back at me from his mirror, looking absurdly white and soft. It had been the same thing after the voyage out to the Indian Ocean. 'Seen Rufus?' one rating had asked another, 'He looks like a f****** kid of 16.' In fact I had then been 20. Now I was nearly 22. Another year and I would have been Milton's age when he noted the subtle theft of his youth by time.

Because of my Westminster scholarship to Christ Church I had had no difficulty in securing a university place. Westminster's connection with Christ Church went back to the time of Queen Elizabeth I, when the scholarships had been founded. I suppose that was one material advantage that I did get from my education there. But, as things turned out, the money was not needed because, together with other ex-servicemen, I had my fees paid by the government.

I was given rooms in Canterbury Quad. It was handsome, with its high eighteenth-century sash windows, though the stone walls, as yet unrestored, were dark and crumbling. We still had coal fires (when there was coal) and the scout still brought us cans of hottish shaving water in the mornings. We had advanced beyond hip baths, however. If I wanted a bath I had to go downstairs and cross the quad in my dressing gown.

I remember going out into the quad on the first evening of my arrival. It was still quite warm and I could see the stars. I thanked whatever powers there were for having brought me there. There would be fresh hurdles in the future. But for the next three years or so, I would be doing congenial work at my own pace, in familiar surroundings and in the company of people with whom I would not have to pretend. I would not have any responsibilities beyond my work except those that I wanted to take on. In the days that followed, this special sense of relief evaporated; but it was strong while it lasted.

Postwar Oxford was of course full of ex-servicemen. There were plenty of students who had come straight from school; but those who had been in the forces predominated; many of them were older than I was. Tutors found themselves dealing with more mature pupils; there were fewer late-night discussions about the meaning of life; the determination to get good, or at least respectable, degrees was more wide-spread. But extracurricular activities flourished as much as ever and, although we looked to the future, there were backward glances as well. *Brideshead Revisited* was already casting its glow.

Coming from a family that was used to academic success (both on my father's side and on my mother's) I wanted most of all to get a good degree. After that I wanted to experiment a bit with politics and with public speaking. I was not ambitious to play an active role in the Oxford

University Conservative Association; but I planned to attend debates, and hoped to become an officer, at the Oxford Union. Before one could attract any attention there and get elected to a committee, one had to sit through many boring hours in thinly attended houses. Eventually, the president would invite one to speak; if one was lucky, this might lead to further opportunities. I was just ambitious enough to persevere in this struggle until the time came when I was asked to make one of the opening speeches. After that, my foot was on the ladder. I used to write my speeches out and try to memorize them, though sometimes I lost the thread and had to improvise.

Because of this political urge, I decided, rather regretfully, that I would not have time to join OUDS (the dramatic society). In my first term, I had two small parts in a Christ Church performance of *Henry VIII*, in celebration of the college's quatercentenary. I was to have been Oberon in another Christ Church play; but Guy Brenton, the old Westminster producer, fell ill with TB. I have never been on a stage since.

I fitted in some less time-consuming activities. I took fencing lessons, as a way of getting rapid exercise, and had singing lessons from a professional teacher. For a couple of terms I ran a rather select and old-established society called the Chatham Club, which met about three times a term to hear distinguished speakers. Mulled claret was dispensed from a jug that was one of the club's few possessions. Funds just ran to a modest dinner beforehand at the Mitre Hotel, where the guest of honour was expected to prefer beer to wine.

I was also a member of the Christ Church Twenty Club, which I think had been going in my father's day. My first experience of it was at the solemn obsequies of a goldfish from Mercury (the pool in the centre of Tom Quad). There was a procession and a French undergraduate conveyed an eloquent tribute from the goldfishes of France. Some time later, there was a debate on a motion with an intriguing triple entendre: 'That a cannon is nothing without balls.' Somebody present had been dining at high table next to one of the canons. When told of the forthcoming debate, the canon sank into deep thought, but never revealed whether he agreed with the motion or not.

As an ex-serviceman, I was 'excused the first public examination'. This meant that I did not have to take Mods (Classical Moderations) and could plunge straight into Greats (*Literae Humaniores*). Greats was — I suppose still is — a seven-term course, which used to enjoy pride of place at Oxford. A graduate from this course was believed to be able to turn his mind to anything, though perhaps with more scepticism than ardour; hence, its particular suitability for senior civil servants. I had always regarded Greats as the culmination of a classical education. But my Greek and Latin had got rusty in the navy and I did not want to spend five terms polishing them up in Mods. The Greats course required some knowledge of Greek and Latin, because a few historical and philosophical authors had to be read in the original; I was just about up to that. Mainly, however, it consisted of ancient history, on the one hand, and philosophy (both ancient and modern), on the other.

I do not regret the time I spent studying Latin and Greek at school. I think it was good for my values and for my grasp of language. But I would have found modern history more congenial if I had been left to my own devices. At Oxford, too, I might have been a better historical, than I was a philosophical, scholar. If I was interested in philosophy it was because I hoped it would instruct me in the mystery of life, or at least help me to get through it decently. These were almost the last things that the logical positivism, then prevalent at Oxford, set out to do. I never quite got to grips with it or found myself in tune with its teachers.

34

However, they taught me enough to get me through my finals and they trained me to think more precisely than I would otherwise have learned to do.

I did not often go to lectures. I preferred to read, in my rooms or in libraries, taking notes the while. Then, in the evenings, I would write essays for my tutors. I did not need to get jobs in the vacations, so I could settle down to a regular routine at home of working between breakfast and lunch and between tea and dinner. I particularly needed to do this in order to study the set books, given my rustiness in Greek and Latin — the speeches in Thucydides are notoriously difficult to understand and translate.

I made a number of friends through the Union. A few of them (Edward Boyle, William Rees-Mogg, Robin Day, Dick Taverne) became well known later. There were other future celebrities like Tony Wedgwood Benn, Kenneth Tynan and Jeremy Thorpe, whom I did not know so well. One of my closest friends, Clive Wigram, had the idea that there was a need for an intelligent right-wing weekly that would do for conservative-minded people what the *New Statesman and Nation* had done for progressive-minded people in the years just before the war. He got together Edward Boyle, Peter Kirk (later a Conservative MP) and myself. We talked to a number of influential people — I remember getting in touch with T. S. Eliot, Quintin Hogg and Ivor Brown — and had some promises of support. But, in the end, the three others had to give priority to more pressing commitments and the venture seemed too risky financially for me to want to take the lead in it. I am the only one of that quartet still alive. Clive, who would have been a brilliant barrister, married the daughter of Sir David Maxwell-Fyfe, but died young when I was in my first post abroad.

Although I was not active in OUCA, I had one or two brief experiences of real politics. I spoke once at a minor political rally in Peterborough. With Peter Kirk, I did some electioneering at Scunthorpe. I did not like telling people who had been through the Depression of the 1930s how they should vote. I have never forgotten one particular call. At first, the house seemed to be empty. Then, suddenly, a fierce-looking, badly crippled man manoeuvred his leg stumps into the room and harangued me on socialist principles. I began to argue with him; but a disabled woman, who was cleaning the house, came in and looked distressed. I took her to be his wife; although she was not, I felt that I was intruding and had no right to be there; if the man himself enjoyed our argument, he showed little sign of it. So, I got away as soon as I decently could, with the feeling that I would never take happily to political canvassing.

I took my finals in my seventh term, at the end of 1948. They lasted a whole week, except for a short weekend in the middle; on the Saturday I swallowed a couple of sleeping pills and had one good night's rest. During the vacation, I came up to Oxford for my *viva voce* examination. It took an hour, which suggested that I was a borderline case; but the questions caused me no anguish. I did get my first, even if it was not by a wide margin. Robin Dundas, my Greek history tutor (he had also been my father's before the First World War) sent me my marks together with his inside information: 'Cheers! I'm glad you equalled your father. An all-rounder, Meiggs says, and your Ancient History really did it (I wonder what about? Nothing I told you!) and the best Thucydides translations that M. saw.' I got my highest mark (alpha minus) for those translations and my next highest for the ancient history paper — the only one with scope for the sort of impromptu generalizations that came easily to me. Latin and Greek prose apart, my lowest mark (beta plus) was for the subject about which I had thought most — moral and political philosophy.

I was to stay on for two more terms to enable me to pursue my Union career and try for an All Souls fellowship.

36

I would never have dreamt of All Souls if my father had not won a fellowship there and if I had not been christened (and my parents married) in its chapel. My best chance seemed to be to stand as a historian, both ancient and modern. I could not get any regular coaching in modern history; but books were recommended to me and Professor Keith Feiling kindly gave me a couple of tutorials. I did manage to read quite a lot during those two terms — they were certainly not wasted — but not enough to give me any depth of expertise; at the same time, it was difficult to keep up with my ancient history. In the event, Tony Quinton was the only successful candidate. Another and I would have joined him, if the fellows as a whole had judged us up to scratch academically. That they did not was a great disappointment, since two people who knew what the examiners had recommended (one of these two was Isaiah Berlin) had been raising my hopes. The older fellows, though not the younger at that time, wanted the college to have a political flavour. Lord Simon, knowing of my Union career, invited me to lunch at the House of Lords and urged me to stand again. But I had other plans by then and thought it was enough to fail once.

I was more successful at the Union. I had served a term as treasurer and stood for the presidency in the spring of 1949. For the first time in the history of the Union, the result of the election was a tie; Rodney Donald and I each polled 196 votes. Peter Kirk, the outgoing president, was very perplexed by this, since there was no rule and no precedent to guide him. It seemed to me that the most sensible arrangement would be for me to stand down and try again at the end of the following term. I could stay on in Oxford till the end of the year, but Rodney could not. This earned me a few golden opinions, though also a comment in one Conservative newspaper to the effect that politics had become too serious a business for gentlemanly gestures. At the end of the Trinity term I stood again and got in by a handsome majority; I came up for a final term — mostly devoted to Union business — in the autumn.

The Home secretary, Chuter Ede, spoke at the main debate during my term of office; R. A. Butler, a cousin of my mother's, spoke against him. At dinner, I told Rab that I was thinking of going into the Foreign Service rather than politics. He did not try to dissuade me; he even suggested that I might have more real power, or influence, as a diplomat than as a politician. He told me that Ernest Bevin, then foreign secretary, had given his friend Gladwyn Jebb a largely free hand. At the debate itself, he was more nervous about the result than I would have expected; I had to reassure him that our method of telling the votes was reliable; I am not sure that it was — but luckily he won.

I had agreed with my father that, when I left Oxford, I would go into his firm until it was clear whether I would be accepted for the Foreign Service and, if so, whether I would make it my career. So I spent over half a year completing my education in Russell Square. During that time I was treated rather like an heir apparent. I began by sharing an office with Peter Du Sautoy, the managing director. Then, I moved on to do some editorial work and to sit in the sales department; I added up figures (pounds, shillings and pence) under the accountant, prepared some advertisements and learned about printing types from the production department. Away from Russell Square I visited a printing works and a paper firm and called on the main London bookshops with one of the travellers. Every week, the directors met in the Book Committee, after an excellent plain lunch cooked by the caretaker's wife, to decide what books to publish. I sat in on those meetings, without being an active participant — except in the lunches.

One of the liveliest parts of my training was a short period that I spent under a lady in the tiny editorial department. Books other than novels were often sent out for an expert opinion at a modest fee. This lady, who separated the wheat from the chaff, read all the novels with immense rapidity. The wheat went on to the directors and their wives; the chaff was cast into the outer darkness. My mentor was bird-like, elegantly dressed, and rather acquisitive; I was afraid that she would seduce me if I gave her a chance.

Faber & Faber did not specifically aim at turning out best-sellers; that was then still regarded as a rather specialized form of publishing. The firm had acquired its reputation in the 1930s through maintaining a high standard of author-ship, particularly in modern poetry, and by producing books in a way that appealed to good modern taste. (This was the doing of Dick de la Mare.) My father would publish a book, even if it were unlikely to make money, so long as he thought that it was good and would enhance the firm's reputation. Of course, the business had to make a profit overall. Apart from its few really successful authors, it relied on standard lines, such as books on bridge, cookery, and nursing. From time to time, one of the directors would have a bright idea — 'Best Ghost Stories', or 'My Best Story', for instance. There was a series called 'The Faber Library' which I think did reasonably well; another series, called 'Rose and Crown', was a failure and short lived.

The sales policy of the firm was geared to this general approach. My father used to claim that his sales director, Mr Crawley, knew exactly how many copies of each book he could safely sell to each bookseller and would never exceed that quota. When I went round with the traveller I think that the initial number ordered, even in a big shop like Bumpus, was seldom more than half a dozen. On the other hand, booksellers kept serious books far longer on their shelves than they do nowadays. There was a much longer period before a book had to go out of print.

Publishers had done well during the war — or would have, if it had not been for the wartime excess profits tax. They were still doing quite well when I was in Russell Square. Harder times were to come; but I did not anticipate them and they did not colour my choice of profession.

I did realize that, in spite of my privileged position, it would be several years before I could expect to be head of the firm. Dick de la Mare and Peter Du Sautoy would each be in charge first. That meant that, at least until I was relatively old, I would not be able to treat the firm as my property, or take time off, in the way that my father had done. I did not worry about this, but it was at the back of my mind.

My father was very careful not to weigh on me during those months. Not that, in the office, he weighed much on anybody. He let people get on with their jobs and was much liked by the senior staff; four of the directors were close personal friends. For the junior staff, I expect he was rather a remote figure. He would be polite to everybody, but I doubt if he knew many of their names. However, there was a pleasant atmosphere in the firm, which spread downwards from the top. People liked working there.

I was half tempted to give up the idea of becoming a diplomat and did not finally make up my mind until the early summer of 1950. Once I knew that I had been accepted, however, I felt committed by the steps I had already taken. About that time, I happened to meet John Christie, my old headmaster, in an Oxford street. He asked me about my plans, though he took care not to influence my decision. I think he felt, as I did, that I had various abilities, yet none that made it obvious what I should do.

In due course, my place in Faber & Faber was taken by Charles Monteith, a fellow of All Souls and a bit older than I was. After his retirement he told me that he never felt completely at home as a businessman. But he was a discerning editor, with good contacts and a high reputation in the literary world. It was due to him, for instance, that the firm brought out Golding's *Lord of the Flies*, after several rejections elsewhere, and went on to publish the rest of his novels.

4
Postwar Whitehall (1950–53)

Postwar austerity still prevailed in the London of 1950. There were stirrings of fashion and luxury here and there, but they were attempts to revive prewar standards, rather than to create new ones. When I started work in the Foreign Office, on £400 a year, I rented an unfurnished room in Upper Berkeley Street, with a separate bathroom downstairs, for three guineas a week. The room was small and I could only fit in a 2' 6" bed. I had no kitchen or refrigerator. My butter was kept in a pottery cooler on the windowsill. Once a week, I fried my meat ration on a gas ring; some evenings I scrambled eggs on it; other times I ate out, inexpensively. Of course I had some social life; but most of my energy went into the office.

Attlee's Labour government was still in control. Abroad, the Iron Curtain seemed impenetrable, while the Korean War menaced any hopes of greater international harmony. Yet, we had emerged quite recently from an exhausting struggle. Although we did not expect too much, I think we took it for granted that things must get better, rather than worse, in time. The instinctive, limited hope was of 'getting back to normal', though without the unemployment and social deprivation of the 1930s.

At the Foreign Office, too, the prevailing wish — at least subconsciously — was the preservation, or restoration, of as much 'normality' as possible. This was natural enough in a country that, though fully aware of relative decline, still had many of the attributes and responsibilities of a great power. The Foreign Service had been reformed and democratized. But the Foreign Office itself still kept, to a remarkable extent, what I suppose to have been its prewar methods and atmosphere.

The actual building, then approached freely from Downing Street, evoked mid-Victorian splendour and authority. The offices occupied by ministers and the permanent under-secretary were and are imposing. Other senior officials could boast portraits and high ceilings. The rest of us were more economically housed; but we walked down the same impressive corridors. At the top of the grand staircase the famous frescoes (forgivable, because painted by a foreigner) showed Britannia teaching her sons the arts of war and peace. Over the private office a smaller fresco enjoined 'silence' on a profession of communicators.

The Locarno Rooms, which have recently been refurbished, were particularly splendid, because they were originally used for receptions. During the war, with the need for more office space, they had been divided by partitions. Sir Roger Makins (later Lord Sherfield) occupied the largest room as deputy undersecretary for economic affairs. Shortly before I joined the service, he was kind enough to ask me to lunch at the Travellers' Club, because he knew my father. Afterwards, he took me back to the office and showed me his room. He seemed to want to know what I thought about it. I thought that, though large, it was not very beautiful, because of the partitions. With youthful insouciance I said that it wasn't bad. He was half-annoyed and half-amused: 'What do you mean by not bad? It's taken me many years of hard work to get a room like this.'

The Northern Department was on the second floor. Its rooms, though built to last, were not architecturally distinguished. The head of the department had a not very large room, alongside a smaller room occupied by his personal assistant and a typist. The assistant head and another first secretary also had small rooms of their own. The lesser fry (known collectively as 'the Third Room') were divided between two medium-sized offices, each with three desks. On the floor above, the registry clerks shared larger and more crowded rooms with the files. We all shared the windows with the pigeons.

The Northern Department covered the Soviet Union, the five 'satellite' countries and Scandinavia. More properly it should have been called 'East and North European Department'. But I believe its title was a survival from Tudor and Stuart days, when two secretaries of state — for the Northern and Southern Departments — divided home affairs and international relations (then largely confined to Europe) between them. Similarly, when I joined the Foreign Office, the Southern Department still survived, though its province had shrunk to the Mediterranean countries.

We needed to wear thick clothes in winter, because we had to work in temperatures lower than is now usual. Some people kept old jackets to work in, to prevent their best suits getting too shiny. A few wore the traditional civil service garb of striped trousers and short black coats. The young and the smart sported bowler hats and tightly furled umbrellas. The bowler hat was making a brief comeback as part of the nostalgia that, at a different social level, inspired the teddy boys.

The young men of the mid-Victorian Foreign Office had been likened to the fountains of Trafalgar Square, because they 'played from twelve to three'. We had to put in longer hours and there was not much playing. We started later than nowadays; I think I used to arrive between half-past nine and ten. This was supposed to allow time for the telegrams to circulate; perhaps it also reflected the social life of prewar senior officials. At lunchtime we regularly took an hour off, to eat in the clubs and pubs of the neighbourhood, and did not feel guilty about taking a bit more, if we had time and were shopping or meeting friends. On the other hand, we worked later in the evenings. I believe I seldom left the office before eight o'clock, sometimes not till half-past eight or nine. At least once a week I took work home and, after a meal, continued with it till midnight. We worked on Saturdays, too, though rather less formally and not always after lunch. However, we were allowed to take every third Saturday off completely, so it was possible to enjoy some long weekends. I can still remember the glorious feeling of liberation that came over me, late one Friday evening, when I was at a dance in a country house and realized that I could look forward to two whole days away from the office.

Most of the work consisted of reading and writing. There were elaborate rules, and more or less archaic formulae, for corresponding with members of the public and other government departments. We were 'directed by Mr Secretary Bevin' (in fact we directed ourselves) to acknowledge or reply to communications. We invited Admiralty or Treasury officials to lay our observations 'before their Lordships', and so on. This Trollopian style was later relaxed. Once mastered, it had its advantages, but it was clearly not in accord with the spirit of the age. Most of my drafting was done in pen and ink; during this first spell in the Foreign Office, I never really learned to dictate. In any case there was nobody for me to dictate to, unless there was time to summon an unknown typist from the pool. By what must, even then, have been an anomaly, the personal assistant, a dignified elderly lady, could not, or at any rate did not, type. She protected the head of department and coped with his boxes and papers. (Once a year, at Christmas time, she asked the young men of the department to sherry in her Kensington flat.) This meant that the departmental typist, a rather haughty-looking beauty, had no time for the Third Room. However, an efficient dictaphone service was available — though I preferred to read into it what I had already written by hand.

Until the merging of the Foreign and Commonwealth Relations Offices, every incoming document was enclosed in a stiff paper 'jacket' with the registry clerk's brief summary of its contents. (Curzon was reported to have spent part of his diligent days correcting these summaries.) Then, it was up to the desk officer concerned to minute his recommendations for action on the jacket and, where necessary, attach draft replies. If he simply initialled the jacket, it would be returned to the registry and might never see the light of day again. If he thought somebody in another department should read the document, he would write the name of this official (or officials) under his own initials. If he wished the document to be returned to him, or to submit it to his superiors, he would write his name in full, under whatever comments or recommendations he thought fit. On the relatively rare occasions when a document seemed likely to rise higher than the department and its undersecretary, an 'ideal minute' might be prepared for the head of department's signature. Sometimes, even when there was no incoming document, the department might need higher authority for a course of action. Here, too, a submission would be prepared in the Third Room, summarizing the problem, together with proposals for action and supporting arguments.

At an entirely different level, ministers and senior officials might reach decisions, on the basis of incoming telegrams, without awaiting departmental submissions. When there were important crises, with political overtones, meetings might be summoned hastily and there might be little time (or wish) to delegate to the Third Room. But relations with most of the countries covered by the Northern Department tended to be frozen, rather than fiery.

The whole system was of course extremely hierarchical —

and no doubt, to a considerable extent, still is. My minutes or drafts reached the head of department (when he needed to see them) through two officials, one of whom felt in honour bound to correct them quite heavily. Between the head of department and the Private Office, there were an assistant undersecretary, a deputy undersecretary and a permanent undersecretary. Like the Third Room, any of these officials could initial papers off, so that they would proceed no further. They would then return to the department, where the initials of a minister or of the permanent undersecretary always aroused some excitement.

Bevin was then foreign secretary, much respected and loved by those close to him. I only met him once, when a colleague introduced me to him in Downing Street. I was deeply impressed when another colleague, who had attended a meeting with him in his official flat, told me how he (Bevin) had personally decided how to handle the matter under discussion after thinking about it in his bath before the meeting. Very occasionally, he would scrawl something in pencil on our submissions. One of his private secretaries would note in the margin: 'The Secretary of State has minuted ...'; then he would transcribe the scrawl in his own neat hand.

The permanent undersecretary was Sir William (later Lord) Strang. Before the 1951 general elections, he warned us to be extremely careful, saying that he had been in the Northern Department at the time of the Zinoviev letter.[*] Edifying advice from two of his predecessors was displayed in framed minutes on the mantelpiece of the neighbouring

---

[*] On the eve of the 1924 general election, the Foreign Office published a letter from the Russian president of the Communist International to the British Communist Party, encouraging sedition. (The *Daily Mail* was known to have a copy.) It may well have been a forgery. It does not seem to have had much effect on the Labour vote; but there was suspicion in some quarters of an establishment plot.

Southern Department's Third Room. One, by Sir Alexander Cadogan, seemed to me to strike exactly the right note of gentlemanly petulance: 'To send a piece of tape like this to the Secretary of State is really quite wrong.' Another, by Sir Orme Sargent, was undated: 'Always put a date on your minutes.'

I was disappointed to find that the tape, used to bundle jackets together, was pink rather than red. One had to learn the correct way of tying it. There was also a correct way of using pins to attach 'flags' to supporting papers, so as to reduce the risk of drawing senior officials' blood. It took time to feel at home with the different methods of circulating more or less urgent papers round the office — pouches, boxes and tubes. Tubes, used for telegrams, were rapid and alarmingly technological, as they emerged from a fearsome network of pipes. Often we achieved still greater rapidity by taking papers to other parts of the office with our own hands and feet. From the outset, the importance of coordination in the work of government was drummed in on us. We had to learn what papers needed to be seen by what other departments in the office and what other departments in Whitehall. There were standard distributions for certain subjects; extra recipients could be added as the need arose. Another routine skill that had to be learned was security classification. The use of 'top secret' was exceptional; 'secret' was quite sparingly used; but there was a temptation to err on the safe side and grade everything else as 'confidential'. There were, of course, rules and definitions. Periodically, we were told to downgrade papers to 'restricted' or even to declassify them.

A lot of attention is paid in the Foreign Office and posts abroad to good, clear, drafting. Perhaps there is, or used to be, rather too much correction of drafts. But the general aim was to avoid obscurity and pedantry, to keep things simple and to prevent clichés taking the place of thought. Sometimes it was not easy to eschew impersonal language when one was writing anonymously or in somebody else's name. But bureaucratic evasions, like 'it is considered that ...', were not encouraged. Even secretaries of state took an occasional interest in the way their officials wrote. Eden had a particular horror of 'it is appreciated', and once had a circular put out telling us never to use 'appreciate' in the sense of 'realize'. In the only conversation I had with Lord Callaghan, when he was Foreign and Commonwealth Secretary, I mentioned in passing that I was fond of drafting. He seemed genuinely pleased and paid a warm tribute to the standard of drafting in the office. Actually, it is not quite true that I was 'fond' of official drafting. At the beginning, at least, it was often a hard slog to master the sort of style that the work required.

It would be misleading to suggest that we wasted much time on the pleasantly archaic forms still in use in the early postwar period. Similarly, it would be a mistake to conclude, from anything I have written, that the pace was leisurely or that business was conducted inefficiently. On the contrary, we were usually fully stretched, working at the double and trying — perhaps just managing — to catch up. There was an unwritten rule that telegrams and other urgent papers should be dealt with on the day of arrival; other papers, including letters from members of the public, should not be delayed beyond three days. Of course, this did not mean that the end result was all that rapid. One way of clearing an in-tray was to send files to other interested departments for comments. I was always unnerved when my in-tray rose above a certain level and would go to rather drastic lengths to clear it. Of course, we all had 'skeletons' — one or two collections of files that were not urgent and required a good deal of disagreeable application. But, it was possible to think of these as occupying a particular limbo, where the normal rules did not apply. The ideal, seldom achieved, was to go home in the evening with an in-tray containing one, or perhaps two, interesting and undemanding files.

During that first spell in the Foreign Office I was personally extremely impressed by the general level of efficiency. I had already picked up business-like habits, was used to brainwork and had worked hard to get a good degree. But, it seemed to me that the standards, as well as the pace, of work were distinctly higher than anything I had experienced at school, at university, in the navy or in my father's publishing firm. This rather awe-struck impression has remained with me to colour my view of the Foreign Office and Diplomatic Service, whatever shortcomings they — like all human institutions — may otherwise have. Naturally, I got used to the atmosphere in time, so that it no longer affected me so keenly. At the outset, even the simplest operations had to be mastered; later on, one could perform these automatically, though there were always fresh challenges.

I did not realize when I was in the Northern Department that the challenges would expand with seniority. I thought that we did the real work in the Third Room. Above us was a dignified area of unruffled decision-making and judicious delegation. To my surprise and disappointment, I found that, as I climbed the ladder, I took 'the real work' with me. I do not quite know what conclusions to draw from this, except that we are all blinkered by our current experience.

Anxiety and stress of course accompanied pressure of work. During the busiest periods I would find myself sleeping fitfully with imaginary problems chasing round my head. Not very long after I joined, I was told to organize a special flight of some kind to Moscow. The head of the department, a good delegator, impressed on me that nothing must go wrong and then left me to it. Because I was inexperienced, I could not fall back on familiar procedure, so I spent a lot of time trying to think of what might happen. It was excellent training; but of course it was not stress free. Whether or not stress sharpens one's faculties (up to a point, it clearly does), I do not see how it can be avoided in jobs where one either has, or feels, responsibility. Most really successful officials have exceptional stamina and can cope with stress. Others have to learn to put up with it and switch off whenever they can.

Considering the amount of time that many people have to spend in offices, it has always surprised me how little seems to be written about the psychology of deskwork. Perhaps it is studied in business schools; but even realistic novelists seem to avoid the subject. Yet offices, as well as homes, can have their dramas. What distinguishes governmental work is that it is all, at least potentially, of public concern and interest. Perhaps mercifully, the public attention span is limited. The dramas gather about the politicians; the civil servants usually remain faceless and anonymous.

We may distrust our politicians, but we are used to having them around. Civil servants are expected to keep their place. They are supposed to be independent enough to offer impartial and objective advice to ministers, yet dependent enough to do what they are told. In an age that increasingly values democracy, anything that hampers it is regarded with suspicion; civil servants are often discounted or ignored because they cannot claim democratic legitimacy.

From a civil servant's point of view, the picture looks a little different. The business of government has to be carried on. Sometimes there are political guidelines; sometimes there are not. When ministers give definite orders, they are sooner or later obeyed. But there is a lot of scope for nuances of interpretation. For that matter, foreign affairs (at least) are seldom a matter of imposing settled policies; both politicians and civil servants are entrapped by the need to react to constantly changing events. Lord Salisbury (Queen Victoria's prime minister) once said something to the effect that, in his experience, small decisions often determined large ones and that such small decisions were necessarily beyond his personal control. The media tend to promote a false idea of government by personalizing what has become — to some extent it has always been — a highly collective process.

Of course, it can be difficult, even for insiders, to feel certain how much political or 'objective' considerations have weighed in any important policy decision, or how much any failures in policy should be blamed on ministers or on their advisers. In the 1950s, the part played by the civil service in bringing the country through the war had to be recognized. (It was not till later that some people began to wonder whether the civil service should be blamed for our economic decline.) There was, as in other respects, a more deferential atmosphere. It was taken for granted that, whatever their limitations, senior civil servants were distinguished, able and experienced people, who had a right to be listened to and whose integrity was beyond suspicion.

There were also far fewer complaints about the 'culture of secrecy' which, like our class system, is supposed nowadays to afflict Britain uniquely. There may be one or two governments that have a more open tradition than we do; but they are few and far between. It is true that we do not yet have a Freedom of Information Act; but I do not know of any country that has a more developed system of parliamentary questioning, both oral and written. This was another technique that the new entrant had to acquire and a lot of time was spent on it. Unfortunately, as I realized later, the demand for information increases when there is a crisis. Yet, it is when there is a crisis that attention ought really to be concentrated on what needs to be done.

We knew that we were there to serve the public and that we were subordinate, through our ministers, to Parliament. But we also liked to feel (at any rate I did) that we served the Crown. At least symbolically, this helped us to keep our balance through changes of government. In 1953, when my appointment to Branch A of the Foreign Service was confirmed, I received a royal commission signed both by the Queen and by Anthony Eden. At that time I was required to be a 'person of approved industry, fidelity and knowledge'. When I eventually became an ambassador, I was credited with rather less plodding qualities. I no longer needed to know much, or to work particularly hard. But I had to have 'wisdom, loyalty, diligence and circumspection'.

Of course, the Queen never told us what to do. But her distant presence was a reminder that we had some permanent interests to protect. From time to time, monarchical pomp enlivened our dignified but rather gloomy purlieus. Rehearsals for trooping the colour could be heard and, through some windows, seen. Sometimes in the summer I walked home by a short cut in St James's Palace; now and then the sentries would present arms to me, rather to my discomfiture, since I did not know how to respond. I thought they must be taking me for an obscure member of the royal family, until a friend suggested that they were misled by my bowler hat into thinking that I was the officer of the guard. He told me that I ought to say 'Good evening, Sentry'. I never had the nerve to say anything at all.

When George VI died in February 1952, we had to go into court mourning. As far as I can remember, there was a fairly short period when we were told to wear black ties and be careful about accepting invitations to dinner. After that, there was a longer period, of half mourning, when grey and mauve took the place of black and our grief could be more restrained. One evening I joined the queue filing around the dead king's lying in state in Westminster Hall. It was simple, but deeply impressive, in the candlelight. The crowd was not overwhelmed with grief; but it was full of respect, both for the man personally and for his office. Later, I passed the funeral procession on my way to work. For a brief moment, I found myself looking into the carriage of the Queen Mother and the two Princesses, all draped or veiled in black, from top to toe.

I do not mean to give the impression that my colleagues and I spent much time wondering about our place in the constitution or who our ultimate boss was. We were being paid to do a job and we tried to do it as we, or our superiors, thought best. I dare say that more training is given nowadays. Then, there was very little. Apart from one or two days learning about the communications system, we picked up experience on the job. I was lucky in overlapping for a few days with my predecessor (Alan Davidson, who later left the service and wrote successful books on Mediterranean cookery). He taught me more than anybody else about office procedures and the particular problems that I would have to face.

I had nearly three years in the Northern Department, during which I occupied three different desks. For the first year or so, I worked in the Soviet Union section of the Third Room. But, I was clearly not any sort of Soviet expert and I was never concerned with Soviet internal or external policy. I was given a number of practical matters on which to cut my teeth. In all of these we had to start from the premise that, relations being basically hostile, the Soviet Union would try to do us down. This involved a kind of chess — a game at which the Russians were famously good.

Financial claims of one kind or another, both public and private, loomed large; some of these went back before the Russian Revolution. There was no hope of getting any money from Moscow. But there were some balances that we might be able to use when we were sure that the Russians could not retaliate effectively. This was one of the central problems, needing much tape and many flags.

Another was the position of the Baltic States. As a wartime

legacy, we recognized Soviet *de facto* control over them, but not *de jure*. The ministers of the three states in London, though not figuring as heads of mission on the diplomatic list, were entitled to certain personal privileges and immunities. As such (if I remember right), they were included in the list that the Sheriff of Middlesex had held since the reign of Queen Anne. We were all rather sorry for these ministers, who had seen better days and strove gallantly to keep their ends up. One of my earliest decisions was taken when the Latvian minister applied for an ivory pass, enabling him, like recognized heads of mission, to drive through the Horse Guards parade into Whitehall. I agonized about whether to submit this request to higher authority. However, greatly daring, I sanctioned issuance of the pass and was much relieved when I heard no more about it.

The difficulties the Soviet authorities put in the way of our embassy in Moscow were a continual preoccupation. British and other diplomats in the Soviet Union were subject to tight travel restrictions, besides being harassed administratively in various ways. The Russian authorities always calculated these nicely; we hoped to be able to get them to ease up a little if we made life more difficult for their own people in London. Our embassy in Moscow came forward with a number of ingenious suggestions and tried to galvanize us into action. We did our best with other government departments, though it was an uphill struggle. It was quite impossible, for instance, to persuade the Ministry of Transport that officials of the Soviet embassy should be denied driving licences, regardless of their competence to drive. In the end, we did impose restrictions on travel beyond a certain radius from Hyde Park Corner. There was not the manpower to police these restrictions properly. But Soviet diplomats were used to restrictions and were thought to be observing them.

There were several dissident Russian groups in London,

distinguished by initials that I have now forgotten. I never met any of them, but we used to get intelligence reports. Once I tried to draw the threads together and submitted an account of their various aims. The head of the department wondered (very reasonably) whether there was any real point in collecting information about such obscure and powerless associations. But the undersecretary said that one never knew: the information might come in useful one day. So, I went on struggling with their initials. There were also nationalist associations — Ukrainian and Belorussian — that occasionally tried to enlist our sympathy. Their representatives were received in the office, though only at the lowest level, which meant myself. I sat with them on a horsehair sofa in the corridor outside the Third Room. I do not recall what we said to each other. It cannot have been very exciting, though of course I used to record it. On my side, there was almost nothing to say. I was (I hope) polite; but I must have been non-committal.

The activities of the Information Research Department have received some publicity recently. We consulted them about the philosophical aims behind Soviet policy and about fellow-travelling organizations set up, or encouraged, by the Soviet government. What little I knew about Marxism I owed largely to material that they circulated. It is easy enough now to think that the West exaggerated the Soviet threat. But it seemed real enough at the time. We thought that the Second World War could perhaps have been avoided if more attention had been paid to *Mein Kampf*.

I used to dream of visiting Moscow. I never had any sympathy with the Soviet government, or with the ideology that supported it. But there was a mystery about that vast country, and its secretive capital, which intrigued, as well as repelled. Perhaps it was a little in the same kind of way that I later dreamt once or twice of working with, or for, Mrs Thatcher in the days when she absorbed everybody's attention. There are places and people that impinge heavily on our lives without our knowing them personally. In the cases of the Soviet Union and of Mrs Thatcher, there was a hint of menace about my dreams. But most of us can dream quite peacefully about meeting the King or Queen; my father, although not a particularly fervent royalist, had a happy dream of George VI coming to his study and calling it 'a nice little den'. I stopped dreaming about Moscow some while ago. I have still never been there; but somehow it has lost its menace and magic for me.

At the end of 1951, I moved to the desk covering the satellite countries. For a few months I had to deal — alone in the Third Room — with the affairs of Czechoslovakia, Poland, Romania, Hungary and Bulgaria. Our missions in the five countries did their best to keep us informed, though their contacts were necessarily limited. Their reports made depressing reading, but there was nothing we could do about it, except when British nationals got into difficulties — and, even then, we could not do very much.

I was glad when, for my last year in the Northern Department, I moved to the Scandinavian desk. The Finland of those days was regarded as semi-satellite, while Sweden remained at a certain distance because of her wartime neutrality. But Norway and Denmark were good friends. However, it was Iceland that gave me most of my work, because of the 'Cod War' fishing dispute.

This dispute brought us into regular contact with the Ministry of Agriculture and Fisheries (and, through them, with the British Trawlers' Federation), as well as with the Foreign Office legal advisers. We all took it for granted that the British view of maritime law was correct and that the Icelanders were in the wrong. At least so far as words and diplomacy went, nobody could accuse us of failing in patriotic support for the British fishing industry. When the British minister in Reykjavik 'went native' and began to argue that the Icelanders had a case, his retirement was either eased or encouraged. I do not now remember enough to form a proper judgement on how the whole crisis was handled. But, looking back, I wonder if we achieved much by our 'my country right or wrong' attitude, even if we were sure of our rightness. Perhaps, we might have ended up with a rather better result if we had accepted earlier that some worsening of our position was inevitable. Whether British trawlermen could have been persuaded of that is another matter.

The Scandinavian desk provided me with my first experience of diplomatic social life. I found myself invited to national days, as well as to small cocktail parties organized by the Foreign Office for Scandinavian visitors. It was nice to have an excuse for leaving the office early, but it was always an effort to clear one's in-tray in time. On one occasion, when I knew that I was late, I reached the top of the stairs before I found that I still had in my pocket a key to a cupboard containing confidential papers. Without thinking, I gave it to a security guard to put away for me. He took it without demur, but promptly informed my superiors. The assistant of the department was deeply shocked; next day he kept shaking his head at me, more in sorrow than in anger, wondering how I could possibly have done such a thing. Luckily the head of the department was less agitated. I do not know whether the incident was recorded as a security lapse on my personal files. I do not think I ever committed another.

My last days in the Northern Department were tinged with the excitement of my first appointment abroad. This was to Baghdad (or Bagdad, as it was then spelled), just in time for the young King's coronation. There were clothes, sheets and tableware to be bought and wine and spirits to be ordered. I chose my first car, a Ford Consul, and was supplied with tropical clothing by a firm called Bakers in Golden Square. I looked up Iraq in all the books of reference I could find, had a few Arabic lessons and wrote to the ambassador, Sir John Troutbeck, to express my delight at joining his staff. There was a mistaken belief in the department that he had two marriageable daughters; so there was some chaff about 'Operation Troutbeck'. I think I was, in some ways if not in others, rather a young 28. I had learned quite a lot in the Foreign Office, but was no more streetwise than when I had entered it.

I was glad to be going abroad and to be able to clear my desk for the last time. I felt that I had passed three interesting and challenging, but not particularly enjoyable, years. Yet, when I think of the Foreign Office with affection, it is the Northern Department of the early 1950s that comes most to mind.

5

Arabs and Franks

The impact of the Middle East on the British imagination is a commonplace. The only non-European countries with an important influence on 'Christendom' belonged to the Middle (or Near) East until comparatively late in our history — not really before the seventeenth and eighteenth centuries. Except for pirate raids, Arab power never directly threatened the British Isles. But of course we took part in the crusades, when Richard I and Saladin struck up a sort of diplomatic and chivalric friendship. Like other European nations we had close trading links with the eastern Mediterranean from quite early times. Then, as our world power grew, the area became of particular strategic importance to us because it covered the nearest approaches to India. Still later, through the exploitation of oil, it acquired a unique economic importance too. Colouring these considerations, at least on the British side, was a particular sentimental attraction some Arabs exerted on some British travellers. This affection, becoming legendary, was strong enough to have a real influence over events.

When I joined the Foreign Service I was quite ready to succumb to Arab charm. However, I turned down an invitation to specialize because, for one thing, my father thought it would lessen my chance of reaching the highest posts. (He would have preferred me to become a political publisher; but, since I was in the Foreign Office, he fancied me as a future permanent undersecretary.) It was reasonable for him

60

to think so then, though I suspect that in fact I might have done better, from a career point of view, if I had been an Arabist. On the other hand, I would probably have had a less interesting variety of posts. It is unlikely that I would have been sent to both of the two European capitals that I enjoyed most.

As it was, I had more exposure to the Arab world than most non-Arabists. I started in Baghdad. When I moved from Baghdad to Paris, Middle Eastern affairs remained part of my work in the Chancery. After that, there was a gap of 14 years. Then, unexpectedly, I was appointed as number two in Cairo. Coming home, on promotion, I spent the greater part of two years representing the United Kingdom on the Euro–Arab dialogue. After that, I went as ambassador to Algeria, an Arab as well as an African power. This makes a total of nearly 13 years, during which my time was wholly, or partly, spent on Arab affairs.

When he invited me to specialize, the head of the personnel department said that, if I did not, I would knock around the world acquiring some general negotiating skills, but without the comfort of any solid expertise. (There was some truth in this, except that it was quite late in my career before I had any chance to negotiate.) Rightly or wrongly, expertise does confer a sort of prestige and confidence; I have often felt the lack of it. If I had specialized in Arabic I would have been sent for a couple of years to the Middle East Centre for Arab Studies in Beirut. I suppose I would have become reasonably proficient in classical Arabic, or its modern equivalent, to the extent of being able to read and write it, if not very fast. That would have provided a basis for talking with educated Arabs. It would not have enabled me automatically to become fluent in the colloquial speech, which varies from country to country; but I would have picked up more of it than I did. Both in Baghdad and in Cairo I took weekly lessons in colloquial Arabic. But, without the classical framework and without daily practice, I never got very far. What I did learn was soon forgotten.

As a MECAS graduate, I would probably have emerged with a rather different attitude to Arab problems than I had when I first went to Baghdad. I was not a died-in-the-wool reactionary; in postwar Britain few people were. During my wartime naval service I had realized that, even if it were right to try to maintain the Raj, it would be beyond our strength. I felt, and still feel, that, compared with many other human enterprises, the British Empire was on the whole a force for good — at least more of a force for good than for evil. But, in feeling this at that time, I dare say I was in a minority. In any case, since the will to stay in India was lacking and since we could have no clear objective if we did stay, there seemed to be no alternative to the Labour government's policy of withdrawal. In the light of it, everybody had to expect that our position in the Middle East would no longer be what it had been.

The question was how far and how fast it had to change. Given our dependence at that time on Middle Eastern oil, there was a case for arguing first that we should continue to play the role of a big power in the Middle East as long as we could. Second, if we were to have any hope of doing this, we could not afford to abandon traditional methods and connections too quickly. We were gradually, sometimes painfully, adjusting to American predominance, in the world as a whole, including the Middle East. But in that part of the world, we still judged ourselves capable, within limits, of independent action.

Against this more conservative approach it was becoming fashionable, both inside and outside the Foreign Office, to press for less British involvement in the external affairs of the Arab countries and less support (or less appearance of support) of their rulers against democratic forces. If I had gone to MECAS and met more educated Arabs, I might have been more inclined to think in these terms. Whether it would have made any practical difference to my work in Baghdad is another matter.

By temperament I have never been a rebel. In those days I was less questioning of orthodoxy than I later became. I was very conscious of the importance of united teamwork if any foreign policy is to succeed. One of the things I thought I had learned from history was that nations can only become — or remain — great through self-confidence and solidarity. I was also young and inexperienced and ready to trust authority, both present and past. So, if I had doubts, I tended to suppress them. This remained my way of thinking so long as it seemed that, at least in the Middle East, we might still have a semi-imperial burden to carry. The Suez crisis came as a great turning point in this regard. Afterwards Britain had to accept second-rank status and revision of older attitudes became inevitable. I got caught up myself in the disbandment of our colonial empire in Africa. When I returned to the Middle East, in 1973, it was in a post-imperial frame of mind.

✳ ✳ ✳

Baghdad (1953–55)

I arrived at Baghdad in a sandstorm. I had sailed in a luxurious Italian ship from Genoa to Beirut, passed the night in a dingy hotel and then caught the Nairn bus (a fruit of Scottish enterprise) at Damascus. The overnight journey had been long, uncomfortable and — in spite of claims to the contrary — far from sandproof. The villa, which I was to share in Baghdad with the Third Secretary Commercial, was not very sandproof either. Our two servants — Ismail, the Kurdish cook, and Hamid, the Arab houseboy — spent the rest of the weekend cleaning it, in an unparalleled and unrepeated burst of activity.

It was a small modern villa near the river, with a little garden, in the district called Karradat Mariam. Like other houses in Baghdad, it had a flat roof. In summer, when the temperature might reach 120° F in daytime shade, we slept on the roof, protected by sandfly nets. When the sun rose, we rose too, and had another hour or so in our bedrooms downstairs. This was of course before air conditioning had become common.

The heat of the six summer months was very wearisome, though one got used to it. We worked six hours at a stretch in the mornings, then went home to a late lunch and a siesta, followed by swimming or tennis and, after that, social life of one kind or another. At midday the steering wheel of the car was almost too hot to touch. In the autumn there was a spell of violent and prolonged rain. Then we settled down to quite a pleasant winter and worked more normal hours.

The embassy offices and the ambassador's residence were next to each other in spacious grounds on the riverbank, near the bridge and a mounted statue of General Maude (an obvious target for nationalist distaste). They were built in a pleasantly old-fashioned colonial style. The Chancery, the 'political' part of the embassy, was grouped around a court-yard and reasonably secure. I had a small office overlooking the river; a rather noisy air-conditioning machine cooled it quite effectively. There was a swimming pool in the grounds and a lot of doves, making mournful noises. My housemate used to drive at them hopefully, saying 'randy brutes'. He never hit them.

I have never been back to Baghdad. But, to judge from television pictures, it must have been much smaller then than it is now. It was stretched along the two banks of the River Tigris; the main part was on the eastern bank, opposite to us. There was one long and heterogeneous street, the Sharia al Rashid, quite a handsome Sunni mosque, a picturesque sukh (bazaar) and some mediaeval building near the Ministry of Defence. But there was very little to show that this had been the capital of the *Thousand and One Nights*.

The British had left their mark here and there, not only in the statue of General Maude. Red double-decker buses crossed the bridge. There were horse races, a British club at Alwiya and an Anglican church. Quite a lot of new building was in progress; before I left, work had begun on a rose-red royal palace near where I lived. At the other end of the scale there were crowded and miserable-looking slums of mud huts. Aesthetically minded foreigners liked to live in the few 'Turkish' mansions that survived on our side of the river, built round small courtyards with a semi-basement (*sirdab*) for coolness in summer. The British School of Archaeology in Iraq occupied one of these. The head of Chancery, my immediate boss, rented another from an Armenian entrepreneur. He was not ideally suited to Baghdad, being musical and rather a dandy; but he found solace in his mansion, where he would listen to Mozart records and watch lights floating down the river after dark. Once, when he came to our villa, he asked me who my Sunday painter was. It took me a few moments to realize it was myself. (I went on being an occasional Sunday painter until I was about 40, when the urge, or the time for it, petered out.)

I became quite a keen Sunday morning gardener. There were two flowering seasons for roses, in the spring and autumn. In the hot weather virtually nothing but faded and dusty zinnias could be grown, and then only by dint of frequent watering. In my second year, there were exceptional floods. The Tigris kept more or less within its banks, but water rose in our lawn and flowerbeds; in my time the roses never recovered. Salination was of course one of Iraq's main agricultural problems. That year, there was a threat to people and their houses too. At the height of the floods they seemed about to overcome the defences on the other side of the river. I drove once to see what was going on. Soldiers were working feverishly by artificial light to build up mounds, with the water outside only a few feet below the safety level. I was careful not to get in anybody's way. But still it was an indication of the British position then that nobody asked me my business.

I have mentioned social life in the hot weather. Oddly enough, I remember more of it then than in the winter. There were dinner parties given by British and other diplomats; we would drink white wine, which had usually turned sour with the heat. My housemate and I used to give dinner parties, too, chiefly for Iraqi officials and their wives. The men were quite glad to have an excuse for drinking alcohol. It cannot have been much fun for their wives, who drank little or nothing and had less English than their husbands did. Sometimes I was asked to Iraqi parties. One would sit around until midnight, drinking whisky, beer or arrack; then everybody helped themselves to food at a buffet table and promptly went home. In the heat (though of course it got cooler as the evening advanced) I would find this very exhausting. Masguf parties were more enjoyable, when a fish known to the British as the 'Tigris salmon' was broiled on the cinders of an open fire and eaten with bits of salad. Another type of social occasion that I enjoyed was, I think, called a *fatiha*. Two or three of us from the embassy would call to express condolences on the death of a prominent Iraqi. Beyond these condolences there was no conversation. We sat around in a courtyard with the dead man's friends, sipping bitter coffee. The atmosphere of peace was deeper than at any Western funeral.

I took more exercise at Baghdad than at any subsequent post. There was swimming at the embassy pool or at the Alwiya club. I used to play bad tennis with the Swiss chargé d'affaires, who was heavier and older than I was. He used to say that I had more cunning, but he had more force; I never felt that we had much of either. Very occasionally, I went out shooting in some wood or copse not far from the city. Again, nobody objected — there was usually nobody there to object. Being a poor shot, I virtually never hit anything. The one exception was when I went sandgrouse shooting with two others. The skill here was in finding the birds. Once found, it was impossible not to massacre a large number of them. We took the corpses home; but eating them was not a gastronomic treat.

I bought a horse, a fine chestnut stallion, recommended by an Iraqi vet. On Friday mornings in winter we went hunting with the Royal Harrthiya hunt. This pursued jackals, not foxes, and had to jump across irrigation ditches rather than over hedges. But, there were a pack of English foxhounds and an English MFH (an architect), as well as Iraqi whippers-in. The Crown Prince, the uncle of the young King, patronized the hunt. Occasionally, he appeared at the meet, looking very elegant in highly polished boots and a pink coat; but he never stayed very long. Junior officers of the police and the royal bodyguard were expected to put in an appearance. At midday, we would all meet at the house of some wealthy Iraqi to eat lamb and saffron rice with our fingers. Whisky flowed on these occasions; we all — both Iraqi and British — enjoyed ourselves very much. In those days, it never crossed my head that this could be a politically incorrect thing to do. Opponents of foxhunting at home were still a largely silent minority. I believe that, later, Iraqi nationalists criticized the hunt as a sign of excessive anglophilia on the part of their royal family; perhaps they were already criticizing it in private. We saw it simply as one way of promoting Anglo–Iraqi friendship. Quite a mixture of Iraqis took part.

I won a short flat race, organized by the hunt, at the Al Mansur racecourse in Baghdad. My groom plunged a penknife into some part of my horse's hindquarters; so, naturally we got off to a flying start. The steward looked at me suspiciously, but was disarmed by my naïve innocence. Unfortunately, I had put no money on myself; but I was presented with an uninscribed Mappin & Webb cup by the King; I still have it, still uninscribed. I had rather fancied myself in a glossy jockey's shirt parading before the admiring or envious spectators; but as so often, there was a sad sequel to my triumph. I had not known what the groom was going to do and of course could not actually see him doing it. So I never reproached him and offered him a modest tip as if nothing had happened. The tip was as much as I thought I could afford; but he rejected it and went about complaining of my meanness. When I heard of this I worried a good deal about what to do. Finally, I gave him a larger tip (which he accepted), moved the horse to a different stable and dismissed him. Although he was not happy about this, I think he understood why.

I got on better with the two house servants. Ismail, a family man, once stole a silver gilt bowl from me when he was short of funds. He told me a cock and bull story about a visiting hawker, who must have seen it on the dining room table. I pretended to believe this, but spoke of the great sentimental value that the bowl had for me and hinted that I might have to call in the police. Some hours later the bowl reappeared. I had to give Ismail a pound or two, since he said that he had paid this to get the bowl back. I think we both knew that the other was not deceived; but honour was satisfied.

Hamid would not have stolen anything from me. His English was even more limited than my Arabic; so it was difficult for us to quarrel with each other. I have a vivid recollection of him looking at the clothes in my wardrobe and saying disappointedly — in Arabic — that they were 'all black'. (I hardly think they were, though they were certainly not very colourful.) But his attachment, as well as Ismail's, was strained when an Iraqi Christian gave me a small white puppy. It followed me around the garden and I cleaned up its messes myself. Perhaps it was this that was too much for Ismail and Hamid; dogs, other than Salukis, are not prized in Arab countries. At any rate, it disappeared and there was another cock and bull story. Upset though I was, there was nothing I could do. I am afraid I was not as grateful as I should have been when an obliging policeman offered me an unattractive substitute.

Travel could be very satisfying in pre-revolutionary Iraq. It is a fascinating country, with its traces of ancient civilizations and its mixture of peoples and creeds. There are Sunni and Shia Muslims; Armenian, Assyrian and other Christians; Yezidis (sometimes called 'devil-worshippers', but really devil-propitiators). There used to be a large Jewish community. There are Kurds in the north and Marsh Arabs in the south. Much of the country is desert, ringed by uplands and high hills; the central part (Mesopotamia) is watered by the two great rivers, Tigris and Euphrates. The remains of Babylon are disappointing, while the Shia shrines at Kerbela and Najef were out of bounds to unbelievers; but there were other monuments to see. The British archaeologists operated in the north, near Mosul, the place that gave its name to muslin. We used to meet Professor Mallowan and his wife, Agatha Christie, on their way through Baghdad. Once they came to lunch with us. Although I had been told that she did not like people to talk to her about her books, I felt I had to thank her for the pleasure she had given me during my school holidays. She was very kind in a motherly sort of way and did not seem put out. Freya Stark stayed with the embassy information officer once during my time in Baghdad. I also met Wilfred Thesiger at the house of a bachelor colleague. He complained about the adoption of slick Western fashions by young Iraqis; he had with him a young Marsh Arab who seemed to have escaped contamination.

I only once did any serious touring in Iraq. I took a week's leave, so that I could drive in my Ford Consul to Sulaimaniya, where a former British vice-consulate was available for rather spartan visits. The young Kurds, swashbuckling around with their baggy trousers and colourful sashes, made a vivid impression. Then I went on to the mountainous northeast of the country, near the Iranian border, where there was a small rest house. On the way down, an unhappy-looking Kurd stopped me, pointing to a wound on his temple. I did my best to wash it with water from a stream and to cover it with some kind of bandage; I hope I did him no harm — he had no distrust. I wondered whether the wound was due to a blood feud. Either on that trip or at some other time, our consul at Kirkuk took me to call on a Kurdish agha, surrounded by his grown-up sons. We sat peacefully, sipping coffee, in a vine-pleached arbour. The agha spoke of a blood feud involving his own family; he pointed to one of his sons as the man who was destined to carry it on.

Apart from that trip, I took my leave in neighbouring countries. During most of my time in Baghdad the state of Anglo–Iranian relations prevented travel to the East. But I once went to Petra with my brother and once joined my sister in Cyprus, still a British colony. I also had a week alone in Jerusalem, when Jordan controlled part of the city.

It will be clear that there were no restrictions on the freedom of movement of British diplomats in Iraq. In a number of ways the British were still in a privileged position. We had administered the country and were thought by many Iraqis to be still doing so, either directly or indirectly. The RAF was encamped in a sort of garden suburb at Habbaniya, not very far from Baghdad. They had an air vice-marshal who, like the ambassador, had an official

Rolls-Royce; a young RAF officer was on the staff of the embassy as the ambassador's ADC. The RAF presence was not allowed to obtrude in the capital; but it was firmly there in the background. The grand old man of Iraqi politics, Nouri Said, was believed to be our friend, or at least to value our potential support. We were supposed to be on the closest of terms with the royal family.

All this inspired a mixture of fear, respect and resentment, which did not prevent good personal relations in particular contexts. I suppose the ordinary Iraqi accepted the British presence as an act of God; perhaps he was inclined to credit us with supernatural power and cleverness. Some Iraqis valued the security we helped to provide, for commercial — or even for patriotic — reasons. But, of course many young, educated Iraqis longed to see the last of us. Even some of our political friends found it useful to treat us as scapegoats. I could not read the local Arabic press, but it was summarized in the embassy. Hardly a day passed without open abuse, usually unfounded and often quite extreme. My Arabic teacher was distressed by this and asked me why we did not do something about it.

In practice, the embassy was scrupulous in not interfering, or trying to interfere, in the internal affairs of the country. If only for that reason it was impossible for us to do anything about the press. We could only hope that Nouri Said and the royal family would keep their nerve and ensure the loyalty of the army and the police until the people as a whole began to feel the benefit of the oil revenues. Nobody ever expected Iraq to be an easy country to govern. Iraqis could be good friends and often had practical shrewdness, but they could also be violent and passionate.

My own, rather superficial, contacts were mainly with officials and professional men. I once met a young man from a landowning family at a British Council party. I think I must have invited him to some gathering at my house. At any rate, he in turn invited the British Council representative and me to spend a night on a cousin or uncle's estate to the south of Baghdad. We had a feast and much arrack; in the morning, before our departure, we found it difficult to do justice to the cold remains. During the feast, our host told me, with the bluntness that Iraqis can sometimes use, that he had not invited me 'for the sake of your blue eyes', but because he thought that supporters of the status quo (he did not use those words) should stick together. The only other time that I stayed with an Iraqi, my blue eyes were not even remotely at issue. I went with a small party from the embassy to inspect an unimpressive UNESCO project. We spent the night at the palace of a wealthy Iraqi wrongly called by the British 'the Emir of Kut'. Of course we were received with much hospitality. There were bottles of expensive scent in our bedrooms and we were provided with a seated dinner, washed down by the familiar heat-soured white wine. The 'emir' was a dignified, quiet, man almost totally absorbed by his small grandson who, by middle-class English standards, was outrageously spoilt. I cannot remember whether I was told, or saw for myself, that the lawns around the house were close-clipped by hand by an army of labourers.

My acquaintance with the royal family was minimal. I put on diplomatic uniform for young King Faisal's accession and, later, when there was a change of ambassador. At one of the 1953 celebrations, the King's voice was broadcast; I was talking to an Iraqi who seemed genuinely impressed by the beauty of his Arabic. It was hardly possible for anybody to hate the King, but he was thought to be too much under his uncle's influence. The Crown Prince, who had been regent, was definitely disliked. He did not have popular manners and was widely regarded (though mistakenly) as a womanizer. In any case, the Hashemite monarchy had been imposed by the British and, in the eyes of Iraqi nationalists, was still heavily tarred by a British brush.

Not long ago I had my hair cut in London by a Lebanese barber who had been born in Iraq. I suppose he was a small boy when I was in Baghdad. He looked back on this pre-revolutionary period as a golden age, far better than anything that had followed. Yet, he was still firmly convinced of the Crown Prince's wickedness.

Sir John Troutbeck was a quiet, modest man, wholly free from any panache; his wife was still less assuming. Whether from taste or policy, they kept low profiles and a distance from the court. The next ambassador, Sir Michael Wright, was more restless and ambitious; his wife, a rich American, looked for a more commanding social role. They developed a relationship with the royal family, which from one point of view seemed right and proper but from another could be criticized as being too obtrusive and too disregarding of nationalist opinion. I think there was some truth in that criticism. But I wonder whether, even if the Wrights had been as discreet as the Troutbecks, it would have done anything to avert the 1958 revolution. I doubt if we could in practice have taken steps to bring about a more 'democratic' system in Iraq. If we had, it would not have remained democratic or people would have thought we were manipulating it. Our position in the country was such that we either had to be powerful (or to appear to be powerful) or to abandon (and be seen to abandon) attempts to influence significantly the course of events. What destroyed the regime was not 'public opinion' as such, but the attitude of a part of the army. Of course, this attitude was influenced by public opinion; but, once formed, it acquired its own impetus and was hardly to be won over by any concession within our power to make.

Apart from internal complaints, the nationalists objected to British influence over Iraqi foreign policy. Here they may have had more justification. In Britain, 1954 had been regarded as a year of successes for Eden's foreign policy. (In the course of them he paid a flying visit to Baghdad; I saw him hurrying through the Chancery courtyard one evening with his private secretary.) The luck seemed to hold when he became prime minister the following year and Iraq joined the Baghdad Pact — together with Britain, Pakistan, Turkey and Iran — against the threat of Soviet aggression. For many Iraqis, however, the pact was fresh evidence of British domination. Yet, to the best of my limited knowledge, the pact was not at first a British invention; it was an initiative of Nouri Said. Certainly, the nucleus of the pact was the agreement that he signed with the Turks in February 1955. I only met Nouri twice, both times briefly. I was introduced to him as a successful jockey and I once had to take a message to him at home. I had no experience of his powers of persuasion. But he was said to be a difficult man to resist.

I was seldom involved in the Chancery, even marginally, in such high matters. The Chancery in an overseas mission is, or was, its political and administrative hub; the head of Chancery was a central figure, like the executive officer of a ship. When the work of any part of the mission became a matter of political importance, the Chancery would almost certainly be involved. It did not follow that its own work was purely political. Any matter that did not come under the specialist departments (the commercial and information departments, the consular section and the defence and other attachés) had to be dealt with in the Chancery. During my time in the service, chanceries tended to become smaller and commercial departments larger. But what remained of the Chancery maintained its traditional role. Until I became an ambassador, I always worked in or over chanceries; I never had any experience of commercial or information work. Yet, during that time, I was only much concerned with local politics in one post. In Baghdad, political reporting and political contacts were the preserve of the 'Oriental Secretariat', staffed by a counsellor and second secretary, both Arabists.

I did not see a great deal of either of my two ambassadors; there was a counsellor, as well as the head of Chancery, between them and me. Like other new entrants, I had been supplied with a book on diplomatic protocol written by Marcus Cheke. It was rather Old World in tone and was not taken too seriously by the progressive-minded; but I tended to take most things seriously and was particularly worried by one injunction. If I saw my ambassador at a cocktail party I was supposed to go up to him, as a mark of respect and in case he might want to send me on some errand. I always found it quite impossible to interrupt the important conversations that the ambassador seemed to be having. Sometimes I hovered, unconvincingly, in his vicinity; at other times I hid myself out of his gaze. Once I became aware that Sir John Troutbeck was staring fixedly at my midriff. I was wearing, under my jacket, a brown and green cardigan knitted by my mother — I had felt cold without it. Next morning, the head of Chancery told me that the ambassador had considered it too 'sporty' for the occasion.

Most of my time was spent on Iraqi development. The Iraqi government received 50 per cent of the profits of the Iraq Petroleum Company, in which British, French and American oil companies held shares. It had been arranged, not long before my time, that 70 per cent of these Iraqi oil revenues would be earmarked for use by the Iraq Development Board, which included a British member (in my time a former official of the Sudan). I suppose this was an instance of British interference in Iraq's internal affairs; but it was not a grievance. Before I left Baghdad, buildings and other evidence of the Development Board's efforts were beginning to appear in parts of the country. This seemed to justify a little optimism, helping to offset apprehension on the political front. It is easy to become cynical as a diplomat, particularly in some of the less efficient parts of the Third World. But our semi-imperial relationship with Iraq encouraged a sort of paternalism. Although I was not starry-eyed, I was genuinely idealistic in my hope that we could gradually help to reduce Iraq's poverty.

In those days, the Iraqis employed a large number of British experts as engineers, port employees, doctors and teachers. There was no overseas aid ministry in Whitehall. A devoted woman working in the Foreign Office recruited many of these experts almost single-handedly. I was her correspondent in Baghdad. We worked on the principle that 'character' (that is, an ability to get on with the Iraqis) was as important as professional qualifications. Periodically, I had to raise with the Iraqi officials the conditions of service of these experts. Once I was instructed to see the Iraqi minister of health about the way in which a medical professor was being treated; we feared this could discourage recruitment. The minister was perfectly calm (not to say obliging); I was perfectly polite (not to say deferential). Later he had a meal with some friends. One of them told the Oriental secretary that he had boasted to them about his manly independence: the ambassador had sent his secretary to browbeat him, but he had refused to be intimidated. There was often this double edge to our dealings with official Iraq.

The British experts themselves were not always models of behaviour. I once had to reassure a talented English teacher who had heard that the embassy suspected him of homosexuality (I do not think the word was mentioned). We did suspect two others; but it was more because they were neo-fascist. The wife of another expert rang me up late one night to complain of her husband's violence and to ask me to come round to deal with it. I must have become a little more streetwise by then; knowing her reputation, I managed to stay clear. One young female doctor, who had insisted on a really challenging job in Iraq so that she could get over a broken engagement, was sent to a provincial town. After the first night she had to be sent home. It was not clear what had happened, but it seemed to have been rather like the experience of the young Englishwoman in *A Passage to India*. She had overestimated her ability to cope with loneliness in a strange atmosphere. I may have been a bit severe, because I felt that money had been wasted and that we had let down the Iraqis. I remember her weeping in my office, unable to substantiate that any Iraqi had behaved badly.

In 1954 (I think), the Iraqi government urged us to send out a really high-powered British expert, who could report to them on the economy as a whole. After much discussion with London, Lord (Sir Arthur) Salter came out, with his American wife. He stayed some weeks and produced a full and sensible report; I never knew how much of it was implemented; I suspect, not very much. What I do recall is my admiration of his and her resilience. They were lodged, as guests of the government, in the Tigris Palace Hotel, on the eastern bank of the river. They had a suite, but it was poorly decorated and furnished and, even after our efforts to brighten it with flowers, it was calculated to dampen the spirits of any Western visitor. However, they took it in their stride and, within a day or two, Lady Salter had the whole of the hotel staff eating out of her hand.

On one occasion, I did stray into Oriental Secretariat territory. I did some research (if not enough) and drafted a dispatch on the Iraqi irrigation system. Historically, there was evidence that whenever there had not been strong central government in the country the system had broken down, with disastrous results for the economy. I think I argued that this was still relevant and that, however extortionate the landowners who controlled the canals, the government was to some extent bound to rely on their cooperation. There was logic in this argument and perhaps there was some practical truth in it. But, of course it ran counter to prevailing views on the need for land reform. Any British representations to the leaders of Iraq at that time would, rightly, have stressed the need for such reform; I suppose it was not very helpful to remind people of the difficulties in the way of implementing it. The Oriental counsellor congratulated me diplomatically on the draft and said he would keep it to append to a dispatch covering a wider field. In fact, I heard no more about it. I think it became a forgotten skeleton in his in-tray.

The Palestine problem was naturally one of our main stumbling blocks. Even friendly Iraqis got heated when the subject came up in conversation with them. I had of course read a bit about the history and, though uneasy about the wisdom of the Balfour Declaration, did my best to justify British policy and practice. I could see that the Palestinians had a real grievance; but I thought that the Arabs ought to accept the presence of Israel and try to make the best of it. It was not till later that I realized the uselessness of arguing with Arabs on these lines.

I experienced some of the realities of the problem when I spent my week's leave in Jerusalem, staying in a hotel near the old city. I was alone and there was no up-to-date map in the hotel. One day I walked out to the British cemetery. At one point on the road there was some rusty barbed wire, but it seemed to serve no purpose and there were no signs. When I got to the cemetery I sat down on a stone bench, in the sunlight, and thought peacefully about life and death. After a bit, I had a feeling of being watched. I looked up and saw a young Israeli soldier behind a wall, pointing his gun at me. We could not find a language we could both speak. Finally, he decided that I was not dangerous, or he became exhausted by the effort of communication, and I was allowed to go.

The next day, not having learnt my lesson, I walked out in the other direction, towards the old Government House. On this route, there was not even any barbed wire. Again I sat down, at the top of the hill, enjoying a superb view of the city. Again my reverie was broken, this time by a small detachment of sweating Arab legionaries, who had toiled up the hill after me. I went back with them to their post in Jerusalem, through small crowds convinced that I was a spy. In the end, a hospitable Jordanian officer gave me a cup of tea and sent me on my way.

I suppose I must have been vaguely aware, on both walks, that I was taking a risk. If so, I thought I would be able to cope with it — as indeed I did. Now, I am inclined to blame this recklessness. Then, I had a feeling of being in some way sacrosanct, of having the right to walk where I liked.

I had two years in Baghdad, including two full summers, before I had any home leave. Romantically, I decided to make the journey by train. This involved taking the Taunus Express from Baghdad to Istanbul and the Orient Express from Istanbul to Paris. I was looking forward to this and was pleased with my wood-panelled cabin; yet I had not been long in it when I realized how tired I was. It was not that I had been overworked in Baghdad; the heat and the way of life must have taken more out of me than I had thought. Despite that, I enjoyed the short break in Istanbul (I met a Kurdish minister of the Iraqi government, who was lonely and took me out to a nightclub); but another break in Paris, at the end of the journey, was a disappointment. When I got home, the feeling of lassitude lasted several weeks, though it cleared for the final month of my leave. As I began to get back a zest for life I heard, to my delight, that I was to be posted to Paris. Better still, I was to go back to Baghdad for two months, so that I would be able to settle my affairs there comfortably, and then fly to Paris direct.

My housemate in Baghdad had become engaged some months before my leave; so I had moved out of the Karradat Mariam villa and taken a still smaller house, with Hamid, now married, as cook/houseboy. He had managed quite well and I was sorry to leave him. I was sorry to have to sell my horse and my car. In other ways, too, I was sorry to leave the city and the people I had known there. But I was looking forward, rather than back, when (still a rather inexperienced air traveller) I caught my flight for France.

Nearly three years later, during my last year in Paris, we heard that the half-expected revolution had taken place. The King and Crown Prince were murdered in the royal palace on 14 July, the corpse of the latter being mutilated, dragged through the streets and hanged. Nouri at first escaped, disguised as an old woman, but was soon taken and put to death. General Maude's statue was destroyed by the mob, while the ambassador's residence was burnt down and the comptroller of his household shot.

It was the end of the old order. It was also the beginning of a new tyranny, far more absolute and unscrupulous.

* * *

Paris (1955–59)

I have always had a friendly feeling towards France. It has usually stopped short of passion; but I did fall gently in love with the country when I lived there. I was still young enough (in my early thirties) to find a different environment exciting. Why I should already have been well disposed is harder to explain. I never visited France till I was 22; I was not very good at French at school and stopped having lessons when I was 14. Neither of my parents spoke good French. However, they had a cultural respect for France and none of the moral prejudices against it that were cherished in some English families. There was a little French blood on both sides of my otherwise entirely English and Welsh ancestry (an early Huguenot bible is still treasured by a cousin). As a boy, I was an avid reader of historical romances; some periods of French history — particularly the

Revolution and the seventeenth century — seemed to have a special glamour. Although I could not speak or understand French easily, I was used to struggling with written Latin and sometimes struggled with written French.

In 1947 I had my first holiday abroad, apart from naval leaves in India and Ceylon. I went with my mother and sister to Rome, Venice and Paris. We were about to visit Versailles when, in the busy Place de la République, I ran for a taxi, looked the wrong way and was hit in the leg by a motorcycle. It was a bad fracture. I had a week in the Hôpital St Louis, in a large ward, where I was jabbed with penicillin every four hours. Then my father came over with funds and took us back to London, where he paid for me to have the best available treatment. It took several months, yet the initial operation in Paris, under chloroform, did not need much correction. I was left with a memory of discomfort, but also of competence and kindness. The experience did not turn me against French food, though it cured me of the notion that it is always and everywhere better than English.

At this time I was a not unfriendly foreign observer. A few years later, when I was learning to speak French, I was drawn closer to the country and wanted — not to be taken for a Frenchman, but to behave in French company in a way that would meet approval. I took with ardour to good French food and drink and began eating cheese before puddings (I still do, if I am offered both). I was even ready to buy French leisure clothes, though I wore English suits to work. There were of course limits to this process of assimilation. One was physical. I have been thought abroad to be Norwegian, German and American; but, so far as I know, never French. I could never find shoes in France to fit my narrow feet, though I could in the USA.

If one feels friendly towards a foreign country as a diplomat, one is naturally more eager for good political relations. I used to hope that, with better education on both sides, there could be a genuine and permanent entente between Britain and France — such close neighbours, so equal in importance and with so much history in common. Now I am less optimistic; for several reasons, the political entente is no stronger, perhaps a little weaker, than it was in the early 1950s. Despite bursts of francophilia and anglophilia, there seems to be a resistance on both sides to a really close association. This might be depressing if it were not that history also suggests that there is a kind of instinctive awareness that hostility between the two countries should not be allowed to go too far, or last too long. It may be that a certain amount of distance between them is necessary for each to keep the special characteristics the other admires, as well as disdains. I became so fascinated by the way in which the two peoples have alternately admired and disdained each other over the centuries that in 1975 I had a book published called *French and English*. (It is now out of print, except in a Japanese translation. Nobody has ever explained to me why a Japanese university should find the book worth translating. Do they identify with the insular English, facing a more civilized continental power?)

Before the war, aspiring British diplomats needed two foreign languages, one of which had to be French, then still called the 'language of diplomacy'. They normally spent a year abroad, picking up these languages at their parents' expense. After the war this requirement was dropped so that candidates from poorer families could enter the service. There was still a test of 'ability to learn' foreign languages, but it was not very rigorous. In my case, my spoken French was so bad that something had to be done about it. The Foreign Office sent me for six weeks in 1951, when I was in the Northern Department, to study French at Tours, then for another month in Paris in 1952. I was and am very grateful for this. I have never been remotely bilingual, but when I was working in Paris and talking French a lot outside the office I did become quite fluent. Apparently the personnel department regarded me as one of the service's better French speakers. I used the language again in Abidjan and Algiers.

At Tours I stayed in the house of a French solicitor (*avoué*), who meted out good local wine temperately at meals. He and his wife took trouble over me, though I felt inhibited and tongue-tied. In the mornings I went to classes at an institute for foreigners. On free afternoons, I explored the chateaux of the Loire and read Balzac novels. It was autumn and I remember day after day of long, quiet, sunshine.

My first night had been spent in a small hotel. The woman who served me my supper was impressed by my diplomatic prospects: 'But you will be a great man!' she exclaimed, not grudgingly but with pleasure. She made me feel that I was embarking on a Napoleonic *carrière ouverte aux talents*. It was an exchange that would have been surprising in England. I also had a rather un-English exchange with M. Combalbert, a language tutor who gave me a few private lessons. He was an immensely courteous and dignified man, with a high room on the ground floor of a handsome town house. In the course of one conversation, we got on to the differences between the nobility and the *grande bourgeoisie* in France. M. Combalbert said mildly that, from his level, he could not properly distinguish these differences. Then he asked me in what social class I would place him. When I hesitated: '*Voyez-vous, Monsieur Faber*', he said, '*Je crois être petit bourgeois*'. Then he stared at the ceiling, while a fly buzzed against the big French window. It was difficult to envisage M. Combalbert as anything less than an exiled marquis. I rallied and suggested that perhaps he was a *bourgeois moyen*. He was not to be fobbed off so glibly; meek, but heroic, he insisted on looking facts in the face.

Next year, in Paris, I found myself in a milieu that was

itself *grand bourgeois*, though in reduced circumstances. My hostess, the elderly widow of a diplomat, was the daughter of a banker who used to send his personal linen to be laundered in London before the First World War. She shared her flat, on the edge of the Faubourg St Germain, with the niece of a well-known right-wing intellectual. The atmosphere was Catholic and semi-royalist, the food good, but economical. In the WC the toilet paper consisted of thin sheets of devotional correspondence penned in violet ink. There were also poodles. One of them had died on the day of my arrival, so I did not meet the elder of the two ladies until she had recovered her poise. I was then a distraction and she threw herself into improving my French. She introduced me to friends, took me to social gatherings and even gave a dinner party for me; the silver was brought out and we sat afterwards in the little-used salon, where there was a portrait by Philippe de Champaigne. She was exactly the right sort of person to help me overcome my inhibitions. During the second half of my stay with her I felt that I had got through a kind of sound barrier and could speak without having to translate first. She tried to teach me the art of kissing hands; but, when I came to work at the embassy, I was told that Englishmen in Paris were not expected to go as far as that.

I flew direct from Baghdad to Paris, with a change of flights at Rome, in October 1955. I left Paris for London in February 1959. Those three years were, without any question, the most enjoyable of my adult life. I did my work conscientiously; but, for the only time in my working career, it was not the most important thing in my life. I suppose that, up till then, I had had a rather serious youth. I had been head boy at my school in wartime; then I had gone into the navy and had to be somebody other than I was. Afterwards, I enjoyed Oxford, but felt bound to get a good degree; I was under strain during my first years in the

Foreign Office; in Baghdad I was a long way from my friends at home. Partly because of circumstances, and partly because of my own temperament, I had never kicked over the traces, as young men are supposed to do. Of course, I do not mean that I had no fun in all these years. Still, I had never quite let myself go. In Paris, to some extent, I did; I went through a phase which, for most people, would have come ten years earlier. There was a contrast between Paris and London at that time, which helped to get me out of my shell. Paris was smarter and more stimulating; London, more innocent than nowadays, was duller and more austere. The French noticed the shabby clothes of English tourists. Englishwomen in Paris found young Frenchmen more amusing than the bowler-hatted escorts they had left behind.

Anybody reading this book will probably guess that my liberated feeling in Paris had something to do with sex. I do not much like reading about other people's sex lives and I do not want to write about mine. We all know that sex can transform life wonderfully, at least for a time; but its mechanics matter less than its emotions — and these are not easily shared. Because of various inhibitions, I had had no sexual relationship before I was 30; that was no doubt unusual but less so than it would be today. Then I began to find celibacy too much of a strain. For the next 21 years or so, I had a fairly active, though rather fitful, sex life. It was not ideal, but it was often enjoyable and sometimes affectionate. I kept it well away from my work, my family and my normal social life. So it has no real place in this book.

At the same time, I wanted to settle down and have children. My father, whom I resembled in some ways, had married a younger woman in his thirties. Hoping to do the same I made two or three quite serious attempts before I turned 40. But, I had left it a bit late and never managed to pull it off. In Paris I was not yet in any hurry; life seemed full of possibilities. My pay had gone up and I had money enough to take young women out to dine and dance; it was the only place where I have found nightclubs pleasurable.

I inherited from my predecessor, who was also a bachelor, a one-bedroom flat in the Rue de Varennes. It was attractive, but too small for entertaining properly. After some months, I moved to the Rue Corneille, where I had two-thirds of a large flat in a late eighteenth-century building round a courtyard. From the salon, which was hung with faded brown and green tapestries, I could see the Place de l'Odeon and the Restaurant Mediterranée, where Princess Margaret was said to have eaten. The salon was always cold in winter because the central heating had to be fed with coal in the kitchen and I could not afford to keep it at full strength. When I was on my own I wore two or three sweaters, as well as woollen underwear; when I had visitors I lit a wood fire. I also inherited a *bonne à tout faire* called Jeanne. She did her best to prevent my moving from the smaller flat, since it took her longer to get to me; but she liked the larger one when she had got used to it. She came from Poitou and was of a certain (uncertain) age. In some ways she reminded me of Proust's Françoise, though she looked frailer. Like Françoise, she could be as hard as nails; perhaps unlike her, she had a soft centre. Once I found her weeping in the kitchen; I comforted her awkwardly, but did not like to intrude on her privacy by asking questions. I did not expect her to be so constantly in attendance as Françoise was; except when I had a dinner party, I only asked her to cook supper for me one evening a week. On the other hand, since she cooked beautifully, I went home for lunch whenever I could. I have never eaten so well before or since. Her cooking was classical but simple and she would go to great trouble to get the best materials. It would not occur to her, for instance, to make a *sauce béarnaise* with anything other than *fresh* tarragon.

As in other places, the people I entertained most were the

officials and others with whom I had work dealings. My married colleagues often preferred to take their contacts out to lunch at restaurants, so that they could talk shop without boring their wives. I got into the habit of calling on people in their offices, while asking them and their wives home so that I could get on closer terms with them. Sometimes, they would ask me back; sometimes not. After all, I was paid to entertain them; they were not paid to entertain me. Apart from official contacts, I got to know quite a wide range of Parisians — some more or less smart, some intellectual, some bohemian — through chance meetings or private introductions. These acquaintanceships were seldom of much direct benefit to my work; but of course they helped me to understand the country. I think I had more real friends in Paris than in any other post, though I am afraid I lost touch with them once I left France. This is one of the sadnesses of a diplomat's — particularly a single diplomat's — life. It is just too much effort to roll an expanding snowball of acquaintance from post to post.

I was asked into all sorts of households, most of them comfortable rather than grand. But I attended grand functions, too, from time to time. The Jebbs entertained the *gratin* more frequently than their predecessors the Harveys, who were reported to have concentrated on the official and professional worlds. I acted as an usher one evening at the embassy, when the smartest Frenchwomen turned out to meet the Queen Mother. I have never seen such dresses — in many cases, I believe, lent for the evening by the big *maisons de couture*. I saw, rather than met, the Windsors at an embassy dinner party. I had the chance of lunching with them; but missed it because it would have meant postponing my leave. (I have kicked myself since for not doing so.) I did go once to Chantilly, for one of Lady Diana Cooper's famous Sunday lunches; there was a splendidly varied collection of guests and she changed her hat three times.

The Chancery offices at Paris are next door to the embassy, in a less historic but still impressive house. John Beith, later ambassador at Brussels, was head of Chancery; he and his wife Diana were very good to me and became close friends. I was the junior member of Chancery, except for the ambassador's private secretary. My desk was in the library, overlooking a lawn that stretched down to the *Champs Elysées*. I shared the room first with Tony Duff and later with Michael Palliser, both of whom became privy councillors in due course.

My chief job was to keep in touch with French officials over a range of foreign policy questions, notably in the Middle East and in Africa. There was of course a tradition of rivalry, even hostility, between Britain and France in the Middle East. This was felt more keenly in Paris than in London: the French believed that, through our fault, they had lost out in Syria and Lebanon. Perhaps it needed reverses to British policy before this feeling could be assuaged. Meanwhile, it was widely reflected in the French press and in right-wing conversation; to a lesser extent, too, in the department concerned at the Quai d'Orsay. They were perfectly correct in their dealings with us, but less positively cooperative than most of their colleagues at that time. There was a well-known journalist, Edouard Sablier who wrote for *Le Monde* and could be quite unpleasantly critical of British Middle Eastern policy. I got to know him a little and found him friendlier than his articles.

The Suez crisis dominated my first year in Paris. In 1953 the Egyptian monarchy had been abolished after a revolution that brought first General Neguib and later Colonel Nasser to power. It might just have been possible for the West to establish good relations with Nasser by abjuring imperialism, disavowing Israel and financing Egyptian development. But violent Egyptian propaganda — very effective in Iraq and in other Arab countries — made London suspicious of Nasser's long-term aims. Eden had cause to feel aggrieved because he had personally taken a political risk in removing British troops from the Canal Zone in the hope of improving the atmosphere. He was also inclined to see Nasser as a mini-Hitler who should be put in his place before he became too strong. The French and the Americans were suspicious, too. The French feared Nasser's influence in Algeria and the Americans objected to his dealings with the communist world. On 19 July 1956, the Americans withdrew an offer to contribute foreign exchange for the Aswan High Dam; the British followed suit. A few days later, Nasser announced the unilateral nationalization of the canal, then owned and controlled by the predominantly Anglo–French Suez Canal Company, and seized their assets.

The ensuing Suez crisis in a sense passed over our heads. Of course, we were deeply interested and read many reports. We might normally have expected to be heavily involved; but, as is now well known, only a handful of people in Paris and London were fully in the picture. Sir Gladwyn Jebb, our ambassador in Paris, had had an unusually brilliant career. His exclusion from this inner circle must have been very difficult for him given that whatever decisions were made were bound to affect Anglo–French relations. He did succeed once in getting the Foreign Office to grant permission for a meeting with the head of the Quai d'Orsay. I had to take a record of it. It was not a productive meeting because neither side seemed adequately briefed; I do not remember any follow-up.

On 26 July 1956, the ambassador was not in Paris. That was the evening when Eden, who had been entertaining the King of Iraq in Downing Street, got the news that Nasser had seized the Suez Canal. I happened to be duty officer. An official in London telephoned me with the news and told me to stand by for possible instructions. I tried to ring the minister (the ambassador's deputy) but, when I was told that he was out to dinner, I did not pursue him. (This earned me a mild rebuke next day.) A couple of hours later another call came through; there would be no instructions that night.

A few days later the initial reaction of the British Labour Party suggested that the country might be able to unite behind firm action. In the days and weeks that followed, however, the impetus behind any such action seemed to run out. It was difficult not to get the impression that the Americans were, more or less deliberately, stringing us along. It was difficult not to resent their doing so, given that the withdrawal of financial assistance for the Aswan Dam, which preceded the nationalization, had been more of an American decision than a British one. I must have seen many of the reports that would have been shown to the Prime Minister throughout the crisis. I find it easy to understand his sense of frustration. But, long before October, I had abandoned any expectation of the use of force.

I was on a ferry from the Hook of Holland to Harwich when I heard that Anglo–French forces had landed at Port Said on 5 November, ostensibly to secure the Canal for international shipping. The Israelis had already occupied Sinai, while the British and French governments had called on both them and the Egyptians to withdraw from the Canal banks. It is politically incorrect to say so now, but I was excited by, and patriotically supportive of, what seemed an instance of Eden's well-known flair. At least events in Hungary seemed likely to distract the Soviet Union. I maintained this view in some heated arguments with friends in Britain. However, I did assume that the operation had been much better thought out than it seems to have been and that the importance of conciliating Arab opinion would be paramount. I supposed that there was some plan for the future of Egypt and that we would make very clear that we were not conniving with the Israelis.

As it was, the operation seems to have been a serious mistake. It was certainly a failure, because it had to be abandoned in the face of international, including heavy American and Russian, pressure. But I am not so sure that it was the massive humiliation that it is sometimes presented as having been. Nor that our long-term prestige was much worse affected than it would have been if we had failed to react at all. One way or another, we were destined to play a more secondary role in Middle Eastern affairs than we had previously aimed to do. From this point of view, and that of any other lingering imperial aspirations, the Suez crisis at least had the virtue of clearing the air.

The French, who had had few of the reservations about the operation that had divided Britain, had every right to feel let down. But their resentment did not immediately surface.

In the aftermath of the Suez crisis, African questions tended to take up more of my time than the Middle East (I have kept these for the next chapter.) I handled United Nations matters as well. In particular, I enjoyed the high-sounding title of UK Permanent Representative to UNESCO. As such, I got to know a few UNESCO officials and occasionally entertained or called on them; I also looked after Sir Ben Bowen Thomas, of the Ministry of Education, when he came over for more serious contacts. Other permanent representatives to UNESCO were important people in their own countries; we could argue that there was no need for stronger British representation in Paris, because London was so close. I was not greatly impressed by the little I saw of UNESCO, though a few people there were trying to make sense of it.

I had a number of Chancery chores, like reading the *Journal Officiel*. There was also a certain amount of more or less cultural work. This included advice on town twinning, dealing with the organization *Le Monde Bilingue* (which wanted all French speakers to learn English, and all English speakers to learn French, and everybody else to learn one or the other) and contacts with the British Council in Paris. Perhaps it was through them that I found myself giving a talk to a largely French audience on the modern English novel. I attended a film festival once at or near Vichy; when I told the *sous-préfet* where my flat was, he exclaimed '*Ah! c'est le Paris de nos coeurs!*' I invited Angus Wilson back to my flat after a lecture he gave at the British Institute; he had an admiring Frenchwoman in tow, who called him 'Maître'; he was a little on edge, but that and recorded extracts from *Don Giovanni* combined to soothe him.

My talk on the modern English novel was (I think) in English. I still have my notes for it, compiled after a lunch with Charles Monteith of Faber & Faber, who filled me in on 'the neo-picaresque novel' (or whatever *Hurry on Down* and *Lucky Jim* were then called). Perhaps I was better qualified for a talk that I gave on the Middle East to a Franco–British association near Toulouse. I had expected that this, too, would be in English; but, about an hour beforehand, the local British consul told me that I must speak in French. There was no time to translate what I had prepared; so I filled my head with phrases and, having keyed myself up, managed to improvise, more or less intelligibly, in French. At least I did not bore people by talking too slowly. As regards the substance of what I said, I knew that my hearers, though anglophile, were likely to hold conservative views on the French role in the Middle East. So, I did my best not to upset them. I felt rewarded when a local reporter described my evasions as an exercise in '*prétérition souriante*'.

Having sold my Ford Consul in Baghdad, I had bought a Morris Minor for Paris, hoping that it would be easy to park; it was black, with maroon upholstery. In it I visited most parts of France. I often drove out to Fontainebleau and other places for Sunday lunch; sometimes I went on trips to Champagne, Normandy or Brittany at weekends. I had a short holiday in St Tropez, just becoming fashionable, and a longer one in Cannes, before rebuilding had destroyed some of its charm. The autoroutes had not yet been constructed. I drove back over the Massif Central, to avoid bottlenecks by the Rhône. Somewhere in Auvergne I gave a lift to a farmer's widow, who told me that it was the first time that an Englishman had 'taken her in hand'.

I learned to ski at Courchevel. I was over 30 and the instructor's cries of *'plus souple, Monsieur, plus souple!'* still ring in my ears. When I heard those cries, I tried to go floppy, with more or less disastrous results; it was only later that I realized that I was meant to bend my knees, not effortlessly but painfully. In my class there was a rather solemn-looking young man who had a job in publishing and had spent some time at Exeter University. He and his wife were on their honeymoon, but did not want people to know it. He turned out to be a La Rochefoucauld and his wife a Rohan — two of the great names of France. They asked me to give them a lift back to Paris. On the way, we spent the night at the house of a great-uncle who had been an attaché in the French embassy at St Petersburg before the revolution.

These trips were all in my spare time. But, I also made two working tours, calling on officials and visiting factories. We were encouraged to do this, now and again, because there was a feeling that, before the war, the embassy had been out of touch with provincial France. I made one tour in southwestern France, stopping at Auch, Tarbes, Lourdes and Pau. The other was based on Dijon. I had chosen that part of France because I wanted to see the Burgundy vineyards. In fact, only one day was devoted to them; but I was served right because it was one of the most exhausting I have ever spent. In the morning, we stopped at one or two

big vineyards and one or two smaller ones in Beaujolais
having a glass at each one. Then the consul chickened out.
went on to a magnificently hospitable lunch with th
Bouchard family at Beaune, after a wine tasting organized
solely for myself. Almost immediately after the lunch, a
about teatime, I was offered port and cakes by the *sous*
préfet and his wife. Then I had to drive back to Dijon fo
dinner with the prefect's *directeur de cabinet*. I felt oblige
by politeness to sip a little of everything. By the end of th
day I was not drunk, but distinctly the worse for wear
weighed down by alcohol, not buoyed up by it.

Even when it was demanding mentally, most of my wor
in Paris was less demanding physically, and seldom stressful
Quite often, when I called on Quai d'Orsay officials, I ha
to brief myself on subjects about which I knew little o
nothing. But the instructions from the Foreign Office wer
always full and the French officials were helpful an
cooperative. We still benefited from Britain's wartim
prestige; people listened to us with respect and at times w
could even give a lead. Besides, during the first half of my
time in Paris, the French as a whole were in a relatively
humble mood. The Algerian revolt had begun a year before
left Baghdad. Inside France, economic modernization wa
progressing, but had a long way to go, while politica
scandals — like the mystery of the *ballets roses* — neve
seemed to be cleared up. There was a book called *A l'heure*
de son clocher which caused quite a stir; I think it wa
written by a Swiss and published in 1955. It pictured France
as living in the past, obsessed by parish-pump concerns
while other countries passed it by.

A slight air of deference towards us in official circles — o
at least an absence of any superiority complex — lasted unti
the latter half of 1957. (This is of course a generalization
rough but perhaps not too misleading.) I was not mysel
expected to follow French internal affairs, but I remember

94

thinking it surprising that there was not more of a backlash after our withdrawal from the Suez adventure. Lord Gladwyn's memoirs, published in 1972, confirm this impression. The atmosphere was still good when the Queen paid a state visit in March 1957. I had nothing to do with this visit, except for a small walking-on part on one or two occasions. I got my diplomatic uniform out of mothballs for a gala evening at the opera. At the end of the performance I had to get to my car, which I had parked in a side street; this meant slipping through the crowd. One woman was impressed by my uniform; a man was more impressed by my lack of transport (*'Il n'a pas de voiture, celui-là!'*) On another evening I was due to attend a reception at the embassy and decided to walk there, for fear of finding nowhere to park. However, before crossing the river, I was blocked by a crowd held back by a policeman. I tried to explain that I needed to get through. The policeman seemed uncertain and the crowd began to take an interest. One woman in particular (I thought of her as Madame Defarge) was vociferous in demanding that I should not be given any privileges. I told her that it was not her business, but the policeman's. The crowd laughed at that and eventually I was allowed through.

Lord Gladwyn records a revival of nationalist feeling. There must indeed have been such a revival, to allow de Gaulle to return to power in May 1958. In the case of our own relations with France, the turning point (never a total reversal of attitudes) came with the row over arms for Tunisia. Tunisia had become a fully independent country in March 1956; in July 1957, Bourguiba became its first president. Much to the annoyance of the French, it obtained a supply of British arms. There were endless toings and froings, in which the Americans were also involved. At one point, our ambassador in Tunis came over to Paris and I had to look after him. He confided to me that, as a rather junior ambassador, it was difficult for him to compete with Jebb, who was one of the Titans of the service. But it was his duty to put the Tunisian point of view and the case for our giving them reasonable (as well as profitable) support.

If there was a worsening in Franco–British relations, it was never such as to affect personal dealings. Nor were these affected by the general's return to power. In 1956 and 1957 he had been widely, almost universally, regarded as a spent force; the ambassador's occasional talks with him seemed to belong to the past, rather than to the future. However, political revolutions can be rapid; almost overnight the unthinkable becomes not only thinkable but fact. Although there were Frenchmen who deplored de Gaulle's return, there were others who welcomed it enthusiastically. Most of the bourgeois whom I knew seemed relieved by the restoration of benevolent authority; one rather rebellious young woman told me that the general made her feel filial.

I had nearly a year to run in Paris under a Gaullist regime. During that time the change made little difference to my life, whether inside or outside the office. As I have already written, my years in Paris were the most personal, the least professional, of my career. It may be partly for that reason that I have so seldom been back there. I could not enjoy Paris now as much as I did then. There are streets in the sixth *arrondissement* where I cannot walk without thinking of things I felt and did 40 years ago. No other place, except perhaps Oxford, has for me such evocative power.

6

Seeing Africa

End of Empire (1955–62)

My next assignment was to the African Department of the Foreign Office. Except for three years in Washington and the Western Department, I worked on African questions from 1955, when I arrived in Paris, to 1969, when I left London for The Hague. I was chiefly concerned with West Africa and had little to do with East Africa, except when I was head of the Rhodesia Political Department from 1967 to 1969. Of course, the whole area had traditionally been of much greater interest to the Colonial Office than to the Foreign Office. But it was during these years — the 1960s and later 1950s — that the former French and British African colonies became independent. The physical maps of the continent did not need much changing; but the political maps were no longer coloured mauve and red.

I suppose the process began with the independence of Morocco and Tunisia in the spring of 1956. I was then in Paris and can remember seeing Moroccan negotiators in traditional dress, when I went out to ride in the forest of St-Germain-en-Laye on Sunday mornings. But these were North African countries, only indirectly ruled by France, and part of the province of the Quai d'Orsay, not of the Rue Oudinot. It was really Ghana, under Kwame Nkrumah, which started the race in 1957. Nigeria followed towards the end of 1960 and Sierra Leone in the spring of 1961.

Meanwhile, Guinea, under Sékou Touré, was the pacemaker on the French side; independent in 1958, it withdrew from the franc zone in 1960. The other French colonies of West and Equatorial Africa became independent in 1960, after a transitional period within the French community, but retained links of various kinds with France.

There were great differences between the territories — in size, in population and in wealth, as well as in attitudes formed by contrasting methods of colonial rule. But of course they were all influenced by what was happening to their neighbours. In the past, the colonial powers had felt that it was enough to keep their territories as separate as possible and to avoid conflict by maintaining civil, though distant, relations. Now they had to know something about each other's plans. There were already quite close contacts between the Colonial Office and the French Overseas Ministry in 1955. These naturally became more frequent as the pace quickened. When I was in Paris I had to make arrangements for meetings, at least one of them at ministerial level. French colonial rule had been more direct and more assimilatory than British; they had been more eager to turn their subjects — at any rate the educated ones — into Frenchmen. But basically, both countries faced similar problems in this part of the world. Some cooperation was essential and, since this was accepted on both sides, there was a friendly atmosphere for it.

Everything happened faster than expected and the time for preparation was continually shortening. One of my duties in Paris was to train three young Africans, two Ghanaians and one Nigerian, in the arts of diplomacy. Each spent a few months there, one after the other, before returning to their burgeoning foreign ministries; one of them was married from my flat. I also had to place the young king of Basutoland (now Lesotho), still in his minority, with my old French teacher, who was thrilled to find herself in charge of '*un prince nègre*. He was a quiet young man, who arrived at the airport clutching a volume of Trollope. I met him again at The Hague when he was an exile there under Dutch protection after the constitution of his country was suspended in 1970. The Dutch allowed me to call on him to pay my respects, but seemed a little hesitant. Presumably, they half feared some intrigue. However, Britain had no ambitions that I could further. My talk with the King was as blameless as the novel he had been reading when I first met him.

Towards the end of my time in Paris, Gladwyn Jebb wanted to make a tour of part of francophone Africa with me in his wake. For some reason, he did not in fact go; but I was sent to make the journey on my own, after I had left Paris to join the African Department. I was away for three and a half weeks in October/November 1959, shortly before the *annus mirabilis* of independence. I visited Togoland, Dahomey, the French Cameroons and the four French colonies of Equatorial Africa (now Chad, Gabon, Congo and Central African Republic). I also had a short stay in Lagos, as guest of the number three in the colonial hierarchy; while there, I visited Ibadan University. From Brazzaville (Congo) I crossed the river to what was then Leopoldville.

It was a fascinating, though necessarily shallow, experience. I met African leaders, including Sylvanus Olympio of Togo, who was assassinated four years later. Being a rarity at that time — the representative, however humble, of a foreign power — I was welcomed by small guards of honour. I called on French colonial officials, who told me that it was time to forget Fashoda (I could not help wondering how many Britons remembered it). British consular officials had mostly made the arrangements for me; there was usually one elegant hotel designed by a French architect, where I stayed. Libreville and Brazzaville had a sleepy sort of charm. In Chad, there were so few educated politicians that the speaker of the National Assembly was a very young man — he looked no more than 20 — in a dazzlingly modish bush shirt.

At Lagos, I was impressed by the atmosphere of colonial efficiency, but also struck by the lack of social contact between rulers and ruled. This was not so much due to racism; it was just not considered part of the job. The governor might invite top Nigerians to garden parties; there was one club with mixed membership; otherwise relationships were in the office rather than the home. My hosts took me one evening to dinner with the (British) attorney general. The other guests were colleagues and bridge-players. They played bridge both before and after dinner; the two who did not play — myself and a young Merchant Navy officer staying with his uncle — had to make what we could of each other's company. Directly after dinner there was a solemn procession of all the men onto the lawn. We stood around the edges, quietly relieving ourselves. This ceremony was known as 'seeing Africa'.

When I got back to London, of course I wrote a report, a rather impressionistic survey with a more detailed appendix; the main part of it was printed and given a wide circulation, including ministers. I had not made any sensational discoveries. But I had been to countries that were then little known in Whitehall, at a time when we could only guess what our future relations with Africa would be. Philip de Zulueta, then Macmillan's private secretary, told me that he had shown the printed report to his master, who had approved. Rab Butler wrote to my father privately to tell him that it would be a help to him and his colleagues. This cannot have been true; but it was nice of him to give my parents pleasure. I had included a well-known quotation from Tacitus. This would not have offended Macmillan or Butler; but I doubt whether, if I were still reporting to the Foreign Office, I would burst into Latin today.

I had a mixture of responsibilities in the African Department. We had to decide what diplomatic missions we ought to establish in the newly liberated countries. At first we thought we might need their votes at the United Nations and that we should try to avoid giving offence by ignoring them. But British interests were sometimes very slight; we had to weigh them against the resources available. I was also involved, as I had been at Paris, in helping to arrange continuing meetings with other powers. We had a session with the Belgians not long before the Belgian Congo became independent in June 1960. The Belgians seemed reasonably confident that order would be maintained; but it was clear that the supply of educated and experienced Africans was dangerously small. In the event, of course, the handover was anything but smooth.

Thankfully, the Belgian Congo problems were not on my particular desk. I did, however, meet Lumumba, the young prime minister of the newly independent country, when he stopped in London on his way across the Atlantic. It was a Saturday; I suppose I was on duty, or simply happened to be in the office, when the report arrived that he would be flying through that evening. The upheavals in Leopoldville were front-page news; so was Lumumba himself. We arranged a press conference at Heathrow and booked a suite at the Ritz Hotel until he could catch his onward flight. Profumo, then minister of state at the Foreign Office, was available to meet him at the airport and take him to the Ritz; I went with him. The press conference passed off reasonably well; so did the drive into central London; Lumumba and his aides were as pleased as schoolboys when the car took us past Buckingham Palace. After a little polite conversation in the Ritz, Profumo took his leave. I remained behind, hoping that things would continue to go quietly.

They did not. The news had of course spread and soon there was quite a big throng of diplomats and journalists in the suite. It had been our idea that the press conference at

Heathrow would give the journalists what they needed and that Lumumba would then be allowed to relax. But nothing could stop their questions or Lumumba's replies. I was the only representative of the Foreign Office present and I had to leave the room in order to make telephone calls about the arrangements. In particular, Lumumba asked me to arrange for a young Belgian woman (it turned out that she was not what she seemed to be) to accompany him on his flight. I managed to get the resident clerk at the Foreign Office to fix this. I also had to brief Profumo on what was happening, since there was always a risk of criticism in the Sunday newspapers. When I got back to the suite I found it in pandemonium; it was in any case getting late. Eventually, I got most of the visitors out and arranged for those that remained, including Lumumba himself, to have a meal in a private room downstairs.

Then I went outside. There were some fascist demonstrators with placards milling around and a few inert policemen, for whom this was simply in the normal course of things. I tried to explain to the policeman in charge how it would strike our visitors, fresh from their troubles at home; but he would not take me seriously. At that point, one of Lumumba's aides looked out and panicked; others joined him and a minor riot developed, which resulted in one policeman losing his helmet. Finally, we sped off to the airport, with a motorcycle escort, shaken but unhurt. Now I had to explain to Lumumba how this sort of thing could happen in London. He answered quietly that, if this sort of thing could happen in London, was what had happened in his own country so surprising? I had not much to say, though the comparison was perhaps not very close. Next day I got hold of the Sunday newspapers. There was a reference to the dictatorial behaviour of 'a young man from the Foreign Office'. At least it was good to know that I could still be described as young.

There was not yet a separate administration in London for overseas aid; there was a feeling that we ought to do what we could to help our former colonies, but the notion of 'aid for aid's sake' had not yet become widely held or politically correct. I returned from my tour, particularly from my brief visit to Lagos, suspecting that overseas aid might become a more important arm of policy than we had previously realized. I thought that, sooner or later, there would have to be a separate administration to control it, though I assumed that it would always come under some Foreign Office control. Meanwhile, so far as Africa was concerned, there was already in existence a body known as CCTA (Commission for Technical Cooperation in Africa), formed by the colonial powers and South Africa and engaged in a number of useful, if inexpensive, projects. Claude Cheysson, halfway through his distinguished career, was its secretary-general from 1957 to 1962. He had a house in Lagos, where he entertained delegates to a CCTA conference in January 1961, soon after Nigerian independence. I attended that meeting, together with my opposite number at the Colonial Office. We discussed, among other things, a small fund for technical assistance, known as FAMA, which had been set up alongside CCTA for the benefit of the newly independent countries. It had a British secretary, Michael Ensor.

I did not see much more of Lagos, during the CCTA meeting, than I had already seen on my tour. Of course, the Commonwealth Relations Office, not the Colonial Office, now controlled British interests there, and they were handled in a different spirit. In the streets, the atmosphere was still relaxed and friendly and I believe it remained so for some time after independence. Later on, it became an unpleasant, even a dangerous, place for foreigners. I cannot write from personal knowledge, for I never had cause to visit Lagos again.

When I retired from the Diplomatic Service and tried to

think what difference I had made, if any, one thing that did come to mind was the unification of the French and British Cameroons. I do believe that I had some personal influence over this — at least to the extent of enabling it to come about more easily than it might otherwise have done. I only had this opportunity because the British Cameroons was a small territory, known to relatively few people in this country and arousing little interest. Since nobody seriously thought that it would be viable on its own, it was more or less obliged to join Cameroon (the French Cameroons) or Nigeria after independence. In spite of the English/French language barrier, the former seemed a better prospect for the southern part of the country — apart from anything else, Nigeria was already quite large enough. But, of course there were sentimental and practical difficulties to overcome; bananas, in particular, were a stumbling block. I dealt with these problems in the Foreign Office more or less alone, though in close liaison with the Colonial Office. I also took part in negotiations on the spot. I liked to think of the two protecting powers pursuing a policy of enlightened cooperation on behalf of their territories (of course both Cameroons had been under the Germans before the First World War). I hope that the British Cameroons have not had too much reason to regret the arrangement. I am sure that any other available solution must have been worse.

One pleasant memory I have of these negotiations is a visit to Buea, the capital of the British Cameroons. I stayed with the commissioner in the former residence of German governors, then still known as the Schloss. It was high up, with a much more refreshing climate than Yaounde (the capital of the French Cameroons); a really beautiful terraced garden had been lovingly created on the slope below it. The ghost of a German governor's mistress, who was supposed to play Chopin on airless nights, was said to haunt the Schloss. I never see ghosts and did not hear her piano, but I did notice that the plug in the WC still bore the legend: '*nicht zu schnell ziehen.*' Good advice, I suppose, for any diplomat anywhere.

Cameroon was already independent, so we had to deal with a French-speaking African minister. He seemed suspicious to start with, but gradually thawed. At our embassy, the Colonial Office undersecretary, who headed our delegation, was naturally given the best (the only good) spare room. I spent a sleepless night with no protection against mosquitoes, having unwisely suggested to my hostess that her house was less horrible than she boasted it was. Next day I made abject apologies and moved to a hotel.

The upshot of our efforts was that, in October 1961, the British Southern Cameroons joined the French Cameroons in a federal republic, after a plebiscite supervised by the United Nations. Following another plebiscite, in 1972, there was a complete union between them; but by that time I was not involved.

South Africa left the Commonwealth in May 1961, after a referendum of the white population the previous October. We had of course been concerned, rather passively, in these developments. Given our disapproval of apartheid, and our wish to conciliate newly independent Africa, we were in fact glad to see the South Africans go.

I believe that, on the whole, the disbandment of our African empire was carried out efficiently, at all levels of government. Full credit has not yet been given for the interdepartmental cooperation that made this possible. British civil servants are at their best when they are given some definite task to achieve within a limited period of time. Certainly, if there were failures, it was not through lack of effort. The process of disengaging from empire had begun in India about a decade before. There, the right overall decision was taken; but it can be, and is being, argued that less haste, and better security arrangements, might have pre-

vented some of the bloodshed that marred independence. I
cannot judge this. In Africa, under very different circumstances, the achievement of independence was more peaceful. We left in a way that did more good than harm to our
reputation.

Of course, things happened later, both in ex-French and
ex-British territories, which seemed to call in question
whether we were right to withdraw, at any rate with such
speed. In India, for all the Hindu/Muslim massacres, we left
behind a government machine that, for several years, had
been extensively Indianized. In Africa, there were fewer
native officials and both they and the native politicians were
less experienced. Ideally, there should have been a slow process of handing over, lasting a generation. But this was never
on the cards. Once the target was set, everybody wanted to
get there rapidly. The emerging African rulers were impatient
for power. The colonial governments wanted full responsibility or none at all.

The history of all this has yet to be fully researched and
written, at least in a form that would allow the general
public to judge whether or not Britain did a good job of
decolonizing. But, I hope I am right in thinking that the
British government as a whole and the Foreign Office as a
part of it will not be found to have blotted their copybooks
too much.

* * *

Abidjan (1962–64)

After three years in the African Department I was appointed
to a West African post. I was not overjoyed, because
Abidjan, though important to the French, was of comparatively little political or commercial interest to Britain at that
time. I consoled myself with the thought that, as number
two and head of Chancery, I would be a bigger fish, though

in a smaller pool. Our embassy covered three other former French colonies, as well as the Ivory Coast — Upper Volta (now Burkina-Faso), Dahomey (now Benin) and Niger. On top of that, the Ivory Coast was prosperous, with its Robusta coffee and its cocoa. Abidjan could be made to sound quite a glamorous sort of place.

I had a pleasant journey out, in March 1962, on board a French ship from Marseilles. We put in at a number of ports round the coast. I think they had all been under French rule, except for Monrovia, which was easily the most squalid. At Dakar I had a cup of coffee with our ambassador, Adam Watson, who had been head of the African Department when I joined it. Without quite being glamorous, Abidjan's appearance was that of a clean and rather beautiful city, widely spaced (in the better parts), with much greenery, and never far from a lagoon. I am sure it is more developed now. But, even then, there were some gleaming modern buildings, including the recently built Hôtel Ivoire.

My predecessor had started up our embassy after independence, before an ambassador arrived. He left me a house in a suburb called Cocody — a three-bedroomed bungalow built quite attractively by a French architect. Except at night, the living room was kept open to the air and abutted onto a small terrace; the bedrooms, and a narrow dining room, could be air-conditioned by separate machines; the modern furniture and bright fabrics were supplied from London. It was an easy country for gardening; almost anything took root, so long as the climate suited it. I had a small lawn, with crotons and hibiscus bushes. There was bougainvillaea on the terrace and small, brightly coloured birds (humming birds, I think, though I was not then a bird-watcher).

Together with the house, I inherited quite a good cook, who came from Dahomey, and a houseboy, who was an Ivory Coaster. There was also a night watchman, part of a protection racket traditionally organized by Upper Voltans.

He was an innocent-looking young man who, spurred on by the cook and the houseboy, did once manage to kill a poisonous black snake in my garage. One evening, when I was on foot and came home later than usual, there was an alarming noise of bells and war cries. It turned out to be the night watchman who, having worked himself into battle readiness, was unable to recognize his employer.

This may all sound mildly idyllic. The disadvantage of the place was its oppressive climate. Roughly speaking, it was damp and hot for ten months of the year; for another month it rained almost ceaselessly; after that there was a short period when it was a little bit cooler and a little bit less damp. It was not for nothing that, in the earlier colonial days, people had talked of the 'armpit of Africa' and the 'white man's grave'. I have a picture in my mind — I do not know how it got there — of two white traders sitting at midday in an upper room at their trading post. The house-boy would know that it was time to serve chop, when an empty bottle of gin clattered onto the courtyard below. The traders drank, at least partly, to ward off disease. I ran less risk of disease and only drank in the evenings.

The damp could wreak havoc on personal possessions. One evening, I found the Dutch ambassador, who lived opposite me, busily polishing his silver. I made a joke out of this secret and delicate ambassadorial occupation; I am afraid that, quite unintentionally, I embarrassed him a little. He should have told me to follow his example. When I got back to London bits of my own silver had to be professionally treated.

It was not just the climate that was oppressive. I am not sure how it was, but, under the brilliant colours, I quite often sensed, or imagined, an undercurrent of menace. Perhaps this was partly a feeling that the French veneer, though attractive and quite thick, was only a veneer. Underneath there was a different, and wholly unfamiliar, sort of culture.

There were not the appearances of poverty and misery to which I had become used in the Middle East and (during the war) in India. In contrast with the tall and finely featured people of the desert countries, like Niger, the Africans of the Ivory Coast were not, to my mind, particularly good-looking. But they were plump and well built; yams and bananas were not difficult to come by. They were also friendly and good-humoured.

There was of course a large French colony. Some of them had a distinctly *pied noir* mentality and my francophilia was occasionally strained. I hardly ever came across my nearest neighbour; but I am sure that he would have felt that I had no right to be there. I once complained about his very noisy dog; his only response was that I should get one myself. I did not see how this would be likely to reduce the noise, but there was no point in arguing. Neither of us could help it when a mutual passion enflamed the turkeys that each of us was fattening for Christmas. One or other of them would try to get over the wire fence, with much beating of wings. When that happened, my turkey's neck would turn an alarming shade of red.

As diplomats, we chiefly came across members of the French-educated African elite. They were courteous and genial, but — except for one or two of the younger ones — it was difficult to get to know them well. It hardly or never occurred to them to ask us home. I tried to get some of them to mine, but they often failed to turn up, either because they were shy or because it was too much of an effort. I was embarrassed when I asked two Africans to meet a newly arrived French cultural attaché and his wife. Neither of them came. I am afraid that the cultural attaché was secretly rather pleased, but of course he was too polite to show it. He turned out to be an expert on the Incas and the Spanish conquest of South America. So we spent the evening discussing that.

The social life of the expatriates — of any nationality — revolved around sticky beach parties, water-skiing and a relatively inexpensive restaurant called the Pam-Pam, with open-air tables. There was an air-conditioned nightclub at the Hôtel Ivoire and a very expensive air-conditioned restaurant, which had oysters flown in daily from France. There was also a small riding stables run by a rather fierce Frenchwoman, who did her best to maintain high standards. She became a little less fierce if you never questioned her authority.

The embassy offices were provisional and not especially impressive. As I had expected, there was little work of much political importance, though we sometimes had to solicit votes at the United Nations or discuss relations with former British African territories. Once, when my ambassador was on leave, Adam Watson asked me to make arrangements for a meeting of British heads of mission from the whole area. When not on leave, my ambassador was quite often on tour. He had started life in the Levant consular service and much preferred travelling in the embassy Land Rover to sitting in his Abidjan office. I shared my own office with a first secretary who had a colonial service background. He, too, did a fair amount of travelling round our four countries and tended to judge the efficiency of their governments by the (physical) state of the markets. I dare say this was as good a test as any.

So, I was quite often left minding the shop and seldom got away from the capital. I did go a couple of times to Dahomey, where there was an honorary British vice-consul. But, I think I only visited the other two territories once. In Ouagadougou, the capital of Upper Volta, the African ministers and officials I met seemed anxious to please, like eager boy scouts. The US resident ambassador had managed to persuade himself that, though the town might *look* one-horse, it was a vital strategic point for air routes. In Niamey

(Niger) I remember a macabre evening in the house of a UN official. It was stiflingly hot; flying insects besieged us and a young Frenchman relentlessly maintained a pornographic monologue.

I cannot pretend that I ever got to know much more about the *real* Ivory Coast than I did about these other three countries. The country is a patchwork of tribes and languages, the nearest approach to a lingua franca (other than French) being the Hausa spoken by travelling salesmen. As far as I knew, the only diplomat with even a smattering of any of these languages was the Belgian ambassador, a clever linguist who had seen better days. He recommended what he called the 'horizontal method' of language study and certainly practised it himself. He asked his number two where I kept my African mistress. His number two, safely married himself, said that he did not think I had one; the ambassador pooh-poohed this, observing that he knew the English and they were never as correct as they seemed.

The Belgian ambassador may have had some idea of what was stirring in the depths of Ivory Coast politics. I doubt if any of the rest of us did. I was friendly with one of my neighbours, a young minister, well educated and from an influential African family. One day, he dropped in at my bungalow on his way home. He was obviously a good deal perturbed; something had happened that he found difficult to reconcile with his French education. He began to disburden himself of it, but then realized that he had better not. I did not press him — it could have made him suspicious and, in any case, I had no need to know.

I had lunch once with James Baldwin, the American black novelist, and with a member of the US embassy who was looking after him. Baldwin was on an African tour, designed to uncover roots. He, too, found that he had been educated into a different world and was not at home in the continent of his origins. He did not quite say so; but it was obviously no easier for him than for me, if anything even more difficult, to understand what had become an alien environment.

The great power in the country was of course, the president, Houphouet-Boigny. He had been a French minister in Paris (I had shaken hands with him there) but had never made the mistake of losing touch with his own people. He had his share of megalomania: his birthplace, where he later built an enormous cathedral, was known irreverently as '*Yamoussoukro les deux églises*'. He kept a tight control of things, though he managed to avoid the reputation of being a cruel tyrant; certainly the Ivory Coast had prospered under his rule and he had ambitions for its future. He hoped that the rest of the world would take Africa more seriously than South America. The Swiss ambassador, who had served there, used to confide sourly to European colleagues that it would be well for Africa if it could be compared with South America at all; I remember feeling that this was a bit harsh. Of course, those were early days and there was still a good deal of post-independence optimism in the air. We Europeans were struggling hard to avoid colonial attitudes and to accept Africans as full equals. It is difficult to convey accurately such changes of mood. Nowadays, perhaps, there is less optimism about all sorts of things, including the future of Africa. But there is also less of a habit of racial superiority.

The pervasiveness of French influence in the Ivory Coast was well known to, and encouraged by, the president, who believed that his country would make more, and quicker, progress that way. Like its politics, the economy of the Ivory Coast had two layers. The bottom layer may have been African; the top layer was French. The top political layer — the world of ministers and diplomats — was not so obviously French, but here too there were usually French advisers in the background. Naturally, the French had to pay for this, through various forms of assistance. It would have been difficult to work out how far their own economy benefited overall. I suppose it must have done; but the maintenance of French influence in Africa, in one form or another, was regarded as an end in itself. We British had no wish to challenge the French in francophone Africa, so long as we were free to do normal business with its governments. Perhaps we too could be accused of 'neo-colonialism' in some of our former territories, though hardly to the same extent. One could argue indefinitely about whether the French or British approach was better, both before and after independence; the territories were too different for valid comparisons to be made. Both powers could point to successes and failures in Africa.

Whatever the differences, there was some feeling of Anglo–French solidarity to balance them. In any case, normal diplomatic amenity would have prevented conflict between our small embassy and the much larger French one. If we had tried to undermine the French they would soon have got to know and could have made things more difficult for us. In spite of our friendly relations, I expect there were people in the French embassy who took the same view of foreigners impinging on their preserves as my dog-owning neighbour. When de Gaulle vetoed our accession to the European Community, the French ambassador could hardly contain his glee. '*Nous sommes en guerre, Monsieur le Chargé d'Affaires!*' he exclaimed at a diplomatic reception. He enquired after '*sa gracieuse majesté*'. '*Toujours gracieuse*', I replied ungraciously.

The British presence was minimal. Shell and Unilever each had a stake in the country; a Frenchman headed the Shell operation; a Cypriot Greek represented Unilever. There was enough trade to justify a junior commercial officer; among other things, I think we must have sold cotton prints, though less than in the past. The British Council financed a

113

young English teacher and we managed to get funds to set up a tiny information centre. I had a consular commission, but hardly needed it; the vice-consul was well able to deal with such consular matters as arose. Coached by him, I did marry one couple and, since it was a unique event, lavished a bottle of champagne on them. They left the country soon afterwards, but sent me a Christmas card.

Most of the other diplomatic missions in Abidjan were on as small a scale as ours, or even smaller. If we counted for more than they did, it was because of our colonial past in that part of the world. With our position in the Commonwealth, and with links elsewhere in Africa, we might still be regarded as an African power.

One traditional and visible sign of our power was provided, on a modest scale, by a naval visit. A rear admiral arrived, flying his flag in a frigate. The ambassador and myself put on white tropical uniform to be piped on board. To my shame, I could not get my cotton glove off in time to shake the admiral's hand, although the ambassador, who had had more experience of gloves, had warned me of the difficulty. Apart from this, I thought that the visit (which had involved quite a lot of preparation) had been a success. So, it was a disappointment when, at a final party, the young flag lieutenant complained to me that it was 'a poor show' that 'the old man' had been kept waiting for several minutes by an Ivory Coast minister. I could not get him to understand that, by local standards, everything had gone like clockwork and that punctuality had not yet become the pride of the African elite. In the end, I lost patience. 'Well, if that's how you take it,' I said, turning to go. 'I'm afraid I do,' he replied, managing to get the last word.

I had quite a short posting in Abidjan, little over two years. Then I left, via London, for Washington. Not long beforehand there was a change of ambassador. The new one thought that I looked run down and told me that he had said so to the Foreign Office. I expect he was right. Although I did not feel ill, I had not thrived on the climate and I was beginning to allow small worries to get me down. Life in Abidjan could be funny and enjoyable; but, the longer I stayed there, the more oppressive it seemed to become.

7

Rebellious Colonies

Washington (1964–66)

I flew to Washington in May 1964, after a short stopover
for briefing in London. The move took me from one of
our smallest embassies to our largest one. Of course, this
was not the only contrast between Abidjan and Washington;
but there were one or two similarities as well. In parts of
Washington, there were as many people of African descent
as in Abidjan, though their complexions were less brilliantly
black. This was one of the first things that struck me.

By now, I was a senior first secretary. Few people outside
the service are as familiar with diplomatic as with military
or naval ranks; so perhaps I should briefly explain the
system as it was in my day. For administrative purposes, the
Foreign/Diplomatic Service was divided into grades, each
with its own salary scale. As an entrant into the senior
branch of the service, I had joined in grade 9 (third
secretary). In Baghdad I had become a second secretary
(grade 7); in Paris, before I left, I was a first secretary (grade
5). These promotions were more or less automatic, given
good behaviour. Thereafter, the pole became greasier. Some
people were promoted to grade 4 (counsellor) earlier than
others. Some never went any higher. I rose to grade 4 when I
became head of a department in London a year after leaving
Washington. I rose to grade 3 when I became an assistant
undersecretary in London in 1975. I hoped to rise to grade 2
for my final post; I never expected promotion to grade 1.

There was little real difference in the sort of work I did as a third, second or first secretary, except that, as I became more experienced, I naturally assumed more responsibility. I had nobody working under me in Baghdad, Paris and Washington. In Abidjan, where I was head of Chancery, I was — as explained in an earlier chapter — responsible to the ambassador for the efficient functioning of the embassy; I was also his deputy. But the staff was very small. In Paris and in Washington the head of Chancery was a counsellor and the ambassador's deputy a minister. In Baghdad — a considerably larger post than Abidjan, but a considerably smaller post than Washington — the head of Chancery was a first secretary, while a counsellor supported the ambassador. In every post, during an ambassador's absences, his deputy — of whatever rank — becomes chargé d'affaires. Ambassadors themselves can be of different grades, from grade 1 downwards.

Until comparatively recent times, ambassadors were few and far between. In all but the most important courts and republics — even in the USA — ministers, who headed legations (not embassies), represented the sovereign. (Of course there were far fewer, even of these, than there are embassies now.) Originally, a minister was a royal servant who might serve his master at home or abroad. Nowadays, ministers at home rule the roost; their poorer cousins abroad are still found as ambassadors' deputies in the largest embassies.

Diplomats must seem to outsiders to be obsessed by their ranks and promotion prospects. This book may suggest that I was no exception. In any organization that employs ambitious people, there will be competition; there will also be rewards, of one kind or another, for those who are successful. Businessmen are just as preoccupied by their salary levels as diplomats are by their ranks.

I suppose that, in all professions that rely on teamwork, one starts by being supervised and ends by supervising others. In between, there may be a period when one is neither supervised nor supervising. I had reached that stage in Washington. I had also reached a stage when I could have dealings with relatively important (though not quite the most senior) American officials. This is the basic business of diplomacy and one gets better at it with experience. One has to learn to be persuasive, to keep clear objectives in mind, to concentrate on what is important; at the same time, one must listen carefully, remember accurately and report correctly. These skills are not as easy to combine as might at first be thought. I felt that, in Washington, I was on my way towards mastering them. I liked living there less than in Europe; but my work gave me more self-confidence than I had had before, or have often had since.

On my arrival, I was put up in a small flat; but I had to look for more permanent accommodation. Eventually, I discovered a small house in Georgetown, which was within my rent allowance, but just large enough to give dinners for eight or six people at one end of a double living room. It also had a garage and a patio garden. It was in N Street which had several handsome houses, including a few from the federal period (1780–1830). My house was built later in the nineteenth century and was not especially elegant, but it had the charm of a Chelsea cottage. When I got there, my landlady's sister had recently died in my bedroom. I did not know this, though I could see from the pink and white frills that it had not been a man's room. I was a bit disconcerted at first when friends rang up asking for her; but she never returned to haunt me. It was a disappointment when, after one year, my landlady wanted to sell the house and I had to move a bit further out to a white clapboard house with a porch and a less urban sort of garden.

I was lucky to have a part-time Italian maid, whose sister had sewn dresses for Mrs Kennedy. She came in for my dinner parties and gave me lunch twice a week — a good excuse for

walk from and to my office. Sometimes, if I was not going
out, she would leave me a beef stew in a Pyrex dish; coming
home in the evening I would add a little Californian red
wine and heat it up in the oven. For some odd reason,
whenever I think of that house, I see myself doing this.

Georgetown is older than Washington, being named after
George II. I was at home there, in a sense, though I hope I
did not let its colonial atmosphere go to my head. (I had a
scrap once with an Irish building worker, who was blocking
the entrance to my garage on a scorching day; but he was
better at bullying me than I was at bullying him.) Apart
from that, being pretty and full of character, the area had
become extremely fashionable; when I had to leave the
house I knew that I would be unable to find another in
Georgetown that I could afford. Of course, it is not the only
beautiful part of the US capital. With its wide avenues,
monumental buildings, greenery and blossoms, Washington
DC is as beautiful a city as any I have seen. It has splendid
musical and artistic resources, too, as well as parks and
cardinal birds. Naturally, it has drawbacks as well. It is too
much a government city; in most of its cultural life (particularly in its theatres and restaurants) it cannot compare with
New York or with the main European capitals. The respectable parts of the city are not made for strolls — they are too
spacious and not exciting enough. (The less respectable parts
may be too exciting. When I was in Washington, women
would not walk in the parks even in daytime.)

There is nothing dull about the climate. The fall can be
very pleasant, if not as spectacular as further north. The
summer is often unpleasantly hot, so hot that there was a
stubborn myth that the British classed the city as a hardship
post. The spring is a bewildering alternation of winter and
summer days. The winter tends to be more extreme than in
England. I once had to put a dinner guest up for the night,
since she could not get home because of a heavy snowfall

while we were eating. Next day, I was driving to work with snow tyres on my car when a hatted man thumbed a lift. He turned out to be a senator. In the first flush of gratitude, he was on the point of inviting me to his house; but then he had a better idea. Putting his hand in his pocket, he came out with a campaign cigarette lighter with his name and portrait. Not being a cigarette smoker, and not needing to vote for him, I am afraid I never found a use for this.

While I was in the States, I had no excuses for leaving Washington on work. But I travelled a bit on leave. I drove up and down the east coast, visited New Orleans, spent a few days in a ranch hotel in North Carolina and had a short skiing holiday in Vermont. Two or three times, I took the shuttle flight to New York for the weekend. Once I went by air and train to San Francisco, where I hired a Ford Mustang and saw something of California. I was impressed and delighted by much of what I saw. But I have to say that on the whole I have enjoyed travelling in Europe more. This may be partly because I am not as fond of American, as of French or Italian, cooking. It is also because, with my interest in history, I prefer things to be weathered, rather than brashly new. Of course, there is much in the States that is not brashly new; but it is not always easy for the rapid traveller to find it out. I did discover more historical traces, particularly up and down the east coast, than I had expected. (Having my head massaged by a black barber in Georgetown took me back to the eighteenth century as vividly as any experience could have done.) As a rule, however, the historical atmosphere is less dense than in Europe — a relief to some, but not to me. Even on the east coast there seems something curiously provisional about the rural civilization. The cultivated land looks less enclosed than in England, though it does not invite trespassers. Once you are off it, and stray from the nature trails, you are in the wild.

Perhaps there was a touch of political prejudice at the back

1. Before the revolution.
On the lawn at the Baghdad Embassy.

2. ABOVE. Before a Royal Harrthiya hunt, Baghdad.

3. BELOW. After the hunt, Baghdad.

4. An outing from Abidjan

5. LEFT. First house at Washington (Georgetown).

6. BELOW. Second house at Washington (47th Place).

RIGHT. The Zamalek house, Cairo.

BELOW. The house in the Hague (Houtweg).

9. ABOVE. Euro–Arab dialogue: the General Commission at Tunis.

10. LEFT. The Algiers Embassy.

13. ABOVE. The boar hunt for the diplomatic corps, Algiers.

14. BELOW. Introducing embassy staff: the Queen's visit to Algiers, 1980.

of my mind. In the sixteenth and seventeenth centuries, when the first Englishmen crossed the Atlantic, my ancestors were Yorkshire yeomen, firmly attached to the Anglican Church. They were not stirred by the religious dissent that prompted much of the colonization of America; nor were they wealthy or important enough to acquire lands there, where they could live more prosperously than at home. Although I value independence of mind, my temperament (whether or not inherited) inclines to acceptance rather than change. In most places and at most times, I find myself siding with governments against revolutionaries.

All this may seem far-fetched. My Old World prejudices had no effect on my work or on my liking for individual Americans. Because of shared language, and some shared assumptions about government and law, it was normally easier to do business with them than with other foreigners. Englishmen often come under the spell of American vivacity and friendliness — though this warmth may strike short-term visitors most. A characteristic I personally found less attractive was that community pressures on middle-class Americans seemed to be very strong; outside the academic world it was harder than in Britain to get away with any sort of eccentricity. I expect I was particularly conscious of this because I was 40 and unmarried.

I gave, and received, a good deal of hospitality. Most of this was exchanged with middle-grade officials, absorbed in their work, their roses and their children's schools. It was fascinating to try to uncover Italian or Scandinavian attitudes under thick American veneers. Occasionally, I was invited to grander gatherings — to political dances graced by the vice-president, where the band always seemed to be playing 'Why Hello, Dolly', or to Georgetown dinner parties where the head of the CIA or Walter Lippmann might be one of the guests. I never got very good at standing for a long time before meals, having stiff drinks, and then sobering up for the rest of the evening. I discovered that sex segregation could be practised in one room as effectively as in two. But, of course, there were 'fun' evenings, too. I was honoured to be asked to join an exclusive old-established society called the Dancing Class. I went two or three times; but most people there knew each other from childhood; I knew hardly anybody and had to go there in evening dress and after dinner, on my own. Once I did go with a woman, whom I had taken to a restaurant beforehand. But we had hardly done a turn round the floor before a childhood friend cut in.

All embassies differ — in size, in atmosphere, in buildings and in functions. The Washington embassy is in a class of its own (I suppose Bonn would have been the nearest parallel at that time). Working there seemed to me less like serving abroad than in a Whitehall department. The ambassador's residence on Massachusetts Avenue is a dignified, though in some ways rather inconvenient, house designed by Lutyens. The embassy offices are housed next door, in a large, impersonal, modern building. Defence and other experts, who did not belong to the Foreign Service, occupied much of this. The Chancery diplomats had box-like offices along one corridor, the counsellors enjoying larger boxes than the first secretaries did. At the end of the corridor, the minister had a fairly large room and the ambassador a larger one. I took over a counsellor's room, but, unusually, I shared it with my secretary. This had at least one advantage. It was in Washington that I finally learned to dictate fluently.

I seldom came across the ambassador personally; it was the minister who held daily meetings. The rest of us were on very good terms and quite often lunched together in the embassy canteen. In spite of this friendliness, I never had as much sense of belonging to the same 'family' as I had in other posts; it was all too large. I stuck to my own job, without much interference or control, and felt less involved than elsewhere in the general business of interpreting the USA to the UK and improving relations between them.

When I arrived, the ambassador was Lord Harlech, a very able man with an attractive wife, but not of course a career diplomat and so not 'one of us'. He was civil to us all, but there was no intimacy. It was the custom for each diplomat to be asked to a lunch at the residence on arrival and departure. In between, we would only be invited if we were needed because of our area of work. This was fully understandable; but it was very unlike Paris and made me feel a little like an upper servant in a noble household. From this point of view, the atmosphere improved when Sir Patrick Dean replaced Lord Harlech — though, so far as I could judge, Harlech was in some ways a better ambassador. The Deans made a good start by sending out Christmas cards to every member of their large staff. We were invited to the residence a little more often, or at least less predictably.

Lord Harlech was supposed to have been appointed to Washington because of his friendship with the Kennedys. I arrived in the aftermath of the Kennedy era, so I never jousted, or watched others jousting, at Camelot. I do not recall meeting President Johnson, who was not a socialite or particularly drawn to diplomats. I suppose the chief internal event in the States during my time in Washington was the failure of the Goldwater campaign. I followed it rather as I would have followed a British electoral struggle, but without feeling any personal involvement. The chief external event was the Vietnam War. Opposition to it was not so intense as it later became, though most of the younger Americans I met seemed to be against it. It must be difficult now for anybody who did not experience the cold war to understand the atmosphere it generated, or to realize fully the extent to which the Soviet Union and the world communist movement had given the West grounds for paranoia. Sincere and intelligent American right-wingers were deeply worried by

the 'domino effect' of communist advance in Southeast Asia
and elsewhere. I think too that, in some quarters, there was
a rather Kiplingesque sense — which Britons might sometimes feel like encouraging — that it was the turn of the
USA to assume the white man's burden. I had no knowledge
of or personal involvement in the problems of Southeast
Asia. But, ten years earlier, I could have identified with this
kind of view. However, as I have suggested in an earlier
chapter, my thoughts on post-imperial policy had loosened
up since the Suez crisis. I became convinced that the Americans ought to get out of the Vietnam War as soon as they
could. Of course, I kept this to myself; it was not my
business and I doubt whether it was the predominant view
in our embassy at that time.

Throughout my life, the special relationship between the
USA and the UK has been a matter of anxious journalistic
concern. How is it doing? Is it stronger or weaker? Does it
really exist at all? In an historical, and in a linguistic/
cultural, sense it is a matter of fact that there is such a
relationship, though its significance will vary and seems
likely to lessen with time. In any other sense it is simply
something that can be invoked, rather like the *entente
cordiale*, when either side finds it useful to do so. As long as
the UK supports the USA in (for instance) the Middle East,
or as long as the USA makes a massive contribution to
European defence, occasions for referring to the special
relationship — under whatever name — are likely to recur.
It is difficult to imagine any situation where London would
not go to considerable lengths to avoid serious conflict with
Washington. But, we should have learned by now that the
Americans will not, and cannot be expected to, subordinate
any important interest or principle to our convenience.

Meanwhile, in most contexts, the less said about the
special relationship the better. The press tends to overesti-
mate the importance of personal relations between leaders.

Even when such relations really do make a difference, they are bound to be ephemeral. When I was in Washington, there were a number of distinguished British journalists about. It seemed to me that occasionally, in their search for stories, they put a harmful gloss on Anglo–American relations. But I dare say that, more often, they got things right. I never met Alistair Cooke; he did not live in Washington and had seen too many diplomats come and go. Henry Brandon had been the Washington correspondent of the *Sunday Times* since 1950; I once met him in the embassy, but he operated at a higher level than mine. In any case, the topics on which I was working seldom, if ever, hit the headlines. I came across Louis Heren, of *The Times*, socially, but he never asked me for information. Similarly, if I became friendly with Boris Kidel of the *Daily Mail*, it was because I practised some Schubert songs with his wife, who was an accomplished pianist.

It so happens that my particular area of responsibility was one in which there really had been an Anglo–American special relationship. To a considerable extent there still was, though this could sometimes embarrass us a little and — perhaps more often — irritate the Americans. My responsibility was in the field of disarmament, nuclear questions and the political aspects of other more or less scientific matters, such as satellites and space. I believe this was the job that Donald MacLean had when, already a spy, he was working in the Washington embassy. At any rate, I still had the same Canadian secretary, who told me that he was the most charming boss she had ever had. She was certainly the best shorthand typist I ever had, immensely quick and accurate. I needed to dictate reports of quite long conversations on technical subjects and it was a great saving of time not to have to do them in draft first. When we were not too busy, she would tell me about her current young man (she must have been twice his age). Or she would keep my spirits up by retailing the latest research, which showed that elderl unmarried men were much more unhappy than elderl unmarried women.

I did not discuss my own sex life with my secretary. I stil thought sometimes of getting married; but, after turning 4C I was more cautious about hurting and being hurt. By th time I left Washington, I realized that I would probabl remain a bachelor. A decade later, when I was appointe ambassador, I reverted to my earlier celibacy. This was les difficult than it might have been because I had contracte kidney disease.

My work in Washington was more specialized than an other work I have done. It was also, in its way, mor intellectually challenging. Although my brother became physics don at Cambridge, I have always been a scientifi and mathematical ignoramus and I was afraid this woul prove a handicap. Passing through London, on my way t Washington, I called on the head of the Foreign Offic department dealing with disarmament. He urged me not t give in and to buy a book on physics. I did so — it wa called *An Approach to Modern Physics* — but, although more or less understood it when I read it, it went in by on eye and came out by the other. (In the same bookshop, picked up *Disarm and Verify* by Sir Michael Wright, m former boss in Baghdad.) Happily, I found that the politica questions posed by disarmament and nuclear power, dif ficult as they were, could be tackled without detaile technical or scientific knowledge. Whatever expertise I di acquire has long since disappeared. For two years of my lif I had to think about matters that have never occupied m mind (at least in any depth) before or since. That mus explain, if it does not excuse, my inability to remember wha kept me busy at this period except in outline.

Disarmament was quite a fashionable subject in the earl 1960s. Lord Harlech himself, as Sir David Ormsby Gore had wrestled with it. The 18-nation committee on disarmament, from which the UN conference on disarmament later developed, had been set up in 1962. In 1963, the USA, USSR and UK signed a treaty banning nuclear tests in the atmosphere, outer space and under water. They looked forward to 'the speediest possible achievement of an agreement on general and complete disarmament under strict international control'. In 1968, when I was back in the Foreign Office, the same three powers signed the nuclear non-proliferation treaty. While I was in Washington there were no such developments; but there was much preparatory work for the non-proliferation treaty as well as discussion of what to do about underground nuclear tests.

I spent a good deal of time pondering on the dangers and advantages of what — either then or later — came to be called 'the balance of terror'. With a world war in the comparatively recent past, we were less preoccupied than people now are by local conflicts. It seemed that, with all its appalling risks, nuclear weaponry would actually reduce mankind's exposure to war — that only a threat to human survival could be expected to stop people fighting. At any rate, it was evident that the greatest risk of a nuclear holocaust would arise if there was no deterrence, if one power alone was in possession of nuclear missiles or could launch a totally effective first strike. In Britain, we had an additional problem; we had to consider whether to retain nuclear weapons ourselves, or whether we could trust entirely to American deterrence to protect us. Of course, we would have to have done so if we had not already been a nuclear power — even as it was, we were heavily dependent on a degree of American cooperation. But no power can trust another to the bitter end and we had to take France's nuclear status into account as well. Weighing these and other arguments, I did not find that I was being pushed beyond my conscience.

Most of my contacts were with the US Arms Control and Disarmament Agency (ACDA); I called regularly on two officials there. Usually, I was acting on instructions from London; sometimes, the conversation would stray further and I would have to improvise. I discovered that the senior of my two main contacts circulated notes of our meetings quite widely to colleagues in other parts of the US government machine. As far as he was concerned, I think this may have been part of a normal bureaucratic process of keeping one's end up. But I was surprised, and rather flattered, to be greeted at a cocktail party as a kind of celebrity by one of the lucky recipients of my thoughts.

I have to admit that the embassy as a whole, at that time, was more concerned with the future of NATO than with the sort of matters I was handling. No doubt, this reflected priorities in the State Department. If only for that reason, I operated on rather a loose rein, except when moves towards any sort of disarmament seemed likely to jeopardize the American project for a multilateral force (MLF). I tried not to make more of a nuisance of myself than I needed. In the end, the meek inherited the earth; the MLF project was abandoned and a non-proliferation treaty was signed.

Now and then I used to discuss disarmament problems with a youngish member of the Soviet embassy. I had been warned that he probably belonged to the KGB. Having had little to do with Russians (except in the Northern Department), and sitting at Donald MacLean's desk, I was nervous about becoming intimate with him; I was afraid that he might discover or imagine some sexual misdemeanour to my disadvantage. I expect my rather excessive caution amused him; he certainly showed no interest in my private life. We talked in our embassy — though not in my office, which would have been against security rules. When I left Washington, I felt I could safely invite him to my farewell cocktail party. I recall him prowling, in what seemed to be a rather dissatisfied way, round my lawn. As he took his leave, he said that he wanted me to know that things I had said to him had made a difference in Moscow. I never knew — still do not know — how seriously to take this.

Lord Chalfont, recently appointed minister of state at the Foreign Office and in charge of disarmament, paid one or two visits to Washington while I was there. During one of them I met the head of ACDA, an urbane patrician, who either was or behaved like, a Southerner. He invited us to a pleasant meal in his Washington club, where he treated us to cooked oysters. Here, too, the atmosphere was almost that of the eighteenth century. I suppose the club catered for the same sort of social milieu as the Dancing Class. People who think that American society is classless are mistaken; they oversimplify, to say the least.

What else do I remember? Occasional contacts with a NASA representative, some talks at the State Department about American forces in Britain (particularly Holy Loch), and some involvement in a projected agreement about satellites. More distinctly, I recall a bilateral US/UK agreement on the civil uses of atomic energy, which I steered to completion together with Frank Panton, a real nuclear expert from the Ministry of Defence. There were different accounts of how much American nuclear development had owed to Britain at the outset; but it had owed something. Since then, the balance had of course been strongly the other way and there was no doubt that we had more to get from the Americans than they from us. At one meeting with American officials, I made an embarrassed and rather emotional reference to the earlier history. I do not know whether this helped or not; I do know that I felt a bit of a fool. However, the American chairman said kindly to me afterwards that it was something that ought to be mentioned. I felt prouder of another intervention when, on my own initiative, I went down to Congress and talked to officers of the relevant committee. They, too, treated me kindly. We knew that there was a feeling about that the British should not be given any preferential treatment; I hope I did something to dispel it. At any rate, the agreement was signed.

In the late summer of 1966, I was appointed assistant head of the Western Department at the Foreign Office. I went home by sea, in a German ship — the only time I have sailed across the Atlantic. I had enjoyed many things in Washington, but I was looking forward to a different kind of work and I hoped that it would not be too long before I was given a department of my own.

* * *

Rhodesia (1967–69)

I only had a year in the Western Department, which I will describe briefly in the next chapter. Then, in 1967, I got my promotion and became head of Rhodesia Political Department. There was still a separate Commonwealth Office in those days and Rhodesia was of course one of its problems, perhaps its main one. I could get to my new office from the Foreign Office without braving the elements; but it was quite a long walk and there was a 'hole in the wall' to get through. It had already been decided that the two departments of state, and the two services, were to merge. Even after the merger, however, there was a tendency to appoint people who had been in the Commonwealth service to Commonwealth jobs. I must have been one of the first people to cross over and I remember being warned by the head of the personnel department to be careful not to tread on Commonwealth corns.

The result of this was that, instead of advancing in a more or less comfortable groove, I found myself as a new boy working not only on an unfamiliar problem, but with unfamiliar methods and unfamiliar people. Even the filing

ystem was different. There was a rather different attitude,
oo. In the Foreign Office, we tended to pride ourselves on a
aard-headed pursuit of British interests. This was not necessarily immoral — British interests, properly understood,
ncluded reputation, peace and honour, even a reasonable
amount of altruism. But on the whole we were not dedicated
o idealistic goals in international relations. The Commonwealth, on the other hand, both when it was predominantly
white and when it became predominantly black and brown,
was always based on shared ideals rather than on power and
nterest. There was often a preference for blurring the
problems rather than sharpening them.

It is fair to say that, by and large, the general standard of
ability in the Foreign Service was higher. Of course there
were notable Commonwealth Office exceptions. A particularly notable one was my undersecretary, Jim Bottomley,
who later became ambassador to South Africa. When he
could see his way clearly, he was one of the most efficient
people I have known. This did not make him a very restful
boss. He would ring me up in the morning and, after saying
something about not wanting to teach his grandmother to
suck eggs, would ask me whether I had thought of such and
such and what we should do to prepare ourselves for it. I
seldom had (though I spent quite a lot of time worrying
about the job). The contingency did not often arise, but he
was right to try to prevent, or minimize, possible disasters.

George Thomson, now Lord Thomson, was the minister
who dealt with Rhodesia — under one title or another —
for most of my time in the Rhodesia Political Department.
He was Commonwealth secretary from August 1967 until
October 1968 and continued to be involved as minister
without portfolio. Towards the end of my time, the responsibility was taken over by the foreign secretary, Michael
Stewart. George Thomas (later Lord Tonypandy) was our
minister of state; he was always pleasant to deal with, but he

followed rather than led. George Thomson was also pleasant to deal with and, though he took advice, could give a sensible lead when needed.

The Central African Federation of Northern Rhodesia, Southern Rhodesia and Nyasaland had been broken up in 1963, whereafter Northern Rhodesia became independent as Zambia and Nyasaland as Malawi. Southern Rhodesia remained a self-governing colony under the effective control of the white settlers who supplied one-sixteenth of the population. Winston Field's Rhodesian Front captured power in April 1963; a year later he was replaced by Ian Smith, who wanted independence on the basis of a constitution approved by a white plebiscite and a consensus of black chiefs. The British government felt unable to grant independence to a minority government resting on so obvious an assumption of white superiority. In November 1965, Smith proclaimed a unilateral declaration of independence (UDI), which in fact amounted to a rebellion. In December 1966, Harold Wilson had talks with him on board HMS *Tiger* with a view to restoring legality. But agreement was not reached.

What made Rhodesia difficult was that its situation was unique. Britain was in a false, almost farcical, position; we still asserted sovereignty over the country, but either would or could do little to enforce it, although we had to deal with people who were predominantly of British stock. We had not been prepared to use — or even to threaten — force against our 'kith and kin'. Mountbatten was supposed to have brought his considerable influence to bear against the use of force; RAF pilots were believed to have a soft spot for a land where many of them had been trained; the prime minister, Harold Wilson, had himself ruled out the use of force. It had become still more unthinkable by the summer of 1967. Economic sanctions had been introduced but, because of evasion through South Africa and Mozambique, were only having a limited effect. There was some internal

African resistance to the regime; as usual there were those who regarded it as a patriotic struggle and others for whom it was disgraceful terrorism; the official line was that we 'deplored violence from whatever quarter it may come'. We still had a governor, Sir Humphrey Gibbs, who was loyal to the Queen. We still had a mission in Salisbury. Neither could do much to affect what was going on. On the Conservative benches in the House of Commons there were a number of active supporters of 'the Smith regime' (as we always called it). They frequented Rhodesia House and lost no chance of attacking any moves to make things more difficult for Smith and his supporters.

I was not personally involved in the enforcement of econ-omic sanctions; this was the concern of the Rhodesia Economic Department, also supervised by Jim Bottomley. Much of the work of my department was constitutional or legal in scope and almost theological in tone. A number of principles had been laid down for the lawful attainment of Rhodesian independence; the most controversial was NIBMAR — no independence before majority African rule. In drafting parliamentary replies, we stuck rigidly to these formulae. There were recurring, and quite knotty problems (for instance in regard to citizenship and divorce), which arose because we could not recognize the actions and decisions of Rhodesian ministers since the unilateral declar-ation of independence. Judges appointed before UDI were not regarded as rebels, provided they had not demonstrated their support for the regime. We spent a lot of time trying to collect evidence showing which prominent Rhodesians were regime supporters. There was a 'stop list' of such persons meant to exclude them from entering this country. Not very long after my appointment, there was a tremendous row when the stop list was used against a former colonial governor. We thought there was no doubt that he — and still more his wife — were sympathetic to the regime. Our evidence was just good enough to enable George Thomson to convince his own supporters in the House of Commons, but a clever lawyer could have demolished it in a court of law. I got very indignant one evening in a restaurant when I heard a loud-voiced young man telling his girlfriend about this shocking treatment of a distinguished public servant by the Labour government. People like that young man refused to recognize the rebellion for what it was. They made it difficult for us to demonstrate to the outside world that, even though force had not been used, the policy of Her Majesty's Government was not hypocritical.

Although I was a head of department, I still had to do much drafting of papers and speeches myself. This was because everything connected with Rhodesia was highly charged politically. Where we were on such thin ice the exact wording could often be vital. Frequently, too, there was very little time. We might get notice of some parliamentary agitation only a few hours beforehand; time was too short for proper hierarchical reflection. Or a ministerial meeting might be called at short notice. In the case of the ex-governor, for instance, I barely had time beforehand to think what ought to be done myself, let alone discuss the problem with others. To defuse the situation, I made the rather obvious recommendation that the minister should set up an inquiry to review the operation of the stop list and should tell the House of Commons so. This was what happened. Jim Bottomley found admirable people to conduct the inquiry and I gave evidence to them in due course. Nothing was achieved, but damage was limited. This would be true of much that I had to do during those two years.

They were two years of hard work and continual pressure, and not only in the office. For the first time in my career I needed a telephone by my bedside. There was never a weekend that was not interrupted by some enquiry or problem, often two or three. Although I approached my work from a British point of view, not a Rhodesian (whether white or black), it was difficult to avoid a feeling of frustration or an instinctive hostility against 'the bad guys' of the regime.

Nobody at that time had very much confidence that sanctions would lead to majority rule, certainly not in the short term. To sweeten the pill, we tried to ensure that any constitution after legal independence would contain effective guarantees for the rights of minorities. Not surprisingly, however, many white settlers had little faith in such guarantees. Most of them seemed to support the regime, tacitly if not actively. There was some support for a moderate party, but it was confined to a relatively liberal minority. We had to brace ourselves for what was known as 'the long haul' (I think it was a phrase of the prime minister's). This was not a very inviting prospect, since even the ultimate outcome remained doubtful. Yet, there was really no practical alternative.

My own solution — never more than a partial solution — was that we should take every opportunity to detach ourselves from Rhodesia and to pursue a policy of disengagement. We should leave it to the blacks and whites there to settle it between themselves. Since we were not prepared to enforce our sovereignty, the honest course was to abandon it. So long as the black majority was excluded from the political process we should continue to do what we could to isolate the country, but as a leading member of the United Nations not as the responsible colonial power. However, I had to recognize that, for different reasons, total disengagement would not appeal either to the Conservative or to the Labour parties in Britain. In any case, our legal advisers insisted that sovereignty could not just be abandoned; it could only be transferred. So I never pushed my view; indeed, I only remember expressing it at one meeting with senior officials, who, I think, regarded it as rather shocking.

However, I did what little I could to lessen the ties between the two countries and to prevent our entering into long-term commitments on Rhodesia's behalf.

The pressures on us were not solely, even mainly, from the British Conservative Party or from white Rhodesians and their friends in this country. At the opposite end of the spectrum, they came, just as passionately, from the left wing of the Labour Party and from other Commonwealth countries. I never visited Rhodesia and never met the two African leaders (Sithole and Nkomo) who were in prison there. But, once or twice I saw black Rhodesians in my office who were connected with the terrorist/patriot resistance to the regime. Of course, I did not incite them to violence. But I could not reproach them too harshly for furthering a struggle that would not have been necessary if we had suppressed the rebellion. I tried not to 'deplore' the struggle too much in public statements. After all, it was one of the main factors that eventually made a settlement of the Rhodesian problem, or at least our disengagement from it, possible.

Sometimes we had to support, and sometimes to resist, action demanded by the regime's opponents at the United Nations. We gave much time to considering the pros and cons of non-economic — for instance, postal — sanctions against Rhodesia. As always, every proposal involved real practical difficulties and other government departments were not always eager to cooperate. It reminded me of our efforts in the Northern Department to impose sanctions on Soviet diplomats.

Before I left the Rhodesia Political Department, I was able, with my undersecretary's encouragement, to secure authority for the closure of Rhodesia House and the withdrawal of our mission from Salisbury. This fitted in with the efforts at New York to isolate Rhodesia and must have contributed to the end of the long haul years later. It also suited my personal bias towards disengagement. I felt a little extra satisfaction because when, some time beforehand, Rhodesia House had hoisted a Rhodesian flag, I telephoned the man in charge there and warned him that, sooner or later, we would find a way of bringing it down. I took this on myself, fully aware of our impotence to do much about it. I was glad when it turned out that my threat had not been entirely empty.

Meanwhile, the Prime Minister had decided that he must make a final effort to reach agreement with Smith. Messages with picturesque code names began to emanate from the Scilly Isles. It often seemed as if, by this time, Harold Wilson found the Rhodesian problem enjoyable rather than frustrating, a relaxing change from domestic strife. It was entirely due to him, not to the official machine, that there was a summit meeting on board HMS *Fearless*, moored alongside at Gibraltar, in October 1968. Jim Bottomley, though doubtful about the outcome, thought that the government had better reach an agreement with the regime, if it possibly could. I was yet more doubtful than him; but, the meeting having been decided, we did what we could to give it a sporting chance of success.

There was a substantial British delegation, which included among others George Thomson, Elwyn Jones, Gerald Kaufman and Marcia Williams, as well as senior officials from the Foreign and Commonwealth Offices. Although the most junior member, I did not feel too peripheral, since I and my department had prepared all the briefs and the prime minister was kind enough to commend them at the first internal meeting of the British delegation. At that meeting I was struck by his courtesy to officials and by his quick grasp of arguments. I was less impressed by his long-term judgement. In order to reach agreement he appeared to be seriously envisaging security guarantees by Britain, which would protect the white minority well into the future. When I had a chance to speak I suggested that, if we ever had to implement such guarantees, we could find ourselves extremely unpopular in many quarters, especially, in Commonwealth and other Third World countries. Surely we did not want to reach agreement only to find the Rhodesian albatross still round our necks. The Prime Minister took this very well and asked for other people's views; what surprised me was that such an obvious point did not seem to have occurred to him before. This was his weak side. Later in the talks he showed his strong side, namely his amazing flexibility and resilience and his ability to keep abreast of rapid developments.

It is difficult now to remember all that took place. Wilson had some meetings with Smith alone, in his cabin. As far as I could gather, both men were friendly and conciliatory. In the earlier talks, on board HMS *Tiger*, there had been some stiffness towards the Rhodesians; this time they were treated more or less as equals. At the full meetings of the two delegations, Smith led his team capably and quietly. There was no attempt to hide the differences between the two sides, but there was at least a superficial assumption that both wanted agreement. At one point, we broke up into small groups to discuss practical details with Rhodesian officials.

I had not slept in a cruiser since 1943, when I had been an ordinary seaman under training as an RNVR cadet. Now I had a cabin to myself, though only one intended for a junior officer. In the wardroom I incurred the disapproval of Denis Greenhill (about to be permanent undersecretary) by calling for a bottle of port or something on the night of our arrival. I had been working very hard for a week and felt I needed bucking up; in any case, I associated wardrooms with alcohol. I do not think I was the worse for what I drank next day. Apart from that, the only relaxation I remember was a swim in the governor's pool, together with Morris James, of the Commonwealth Office, and Michael Palliser, then Wilson's Foreign Office secretary.

One or two scandalous (not *very* scandalous) stories circulated about Marcia Williams and her supposedly high-
handed treatment of the Prime Minister. The funniest
episode — I wish I had a tape recording of it — was quite a
long discussion by the British delegation of arrangements for
divine service on Sunday morning. Wilson wanted to read
one lesson and to get Smith to read the other. His parliamentary private secretary was appalled at this suggestion,
which could apparently rock the Labour Party to its foun-
dations. 'It would be political dynamite, Prime Minister,' he
insisted, in an agitated Welsh accent. Finally, it was decided
that the captain should read both lessons.

One of the main sticking points — I think it may have
been *the* sticking point — was the question of whether the
Judicial Committee of the Privy Council, sitting in London,
should continue to have jurisdiction over the Rhodesian
constitution after independence. Smith and his colleagues
would not accept this. In my department we had always
considered it a rather theoretical safeguard, likely to prove
of little value in practice when conflict arose. However, the
Lord Chancellor was apparently very reluctant to let it go.
He was telephoned by Elwyn Jones (as Attorney General)
and I believe made it clear that he and other members of the
Cabinet could not endorse a settlement that gave the Judicial
Committee no place in Rhodesia's future. For what it is
worth, my impression at the time was that it was this, as
much as anything, that made the Prime Minister decide
against any immediate deal.

On the last day, we had a meeting of the British delegation
a few minutes before a full session with the Rhodesians was
due. We seemed to be in confusion and disarray; but Harold
Wilson stayed calm. In accordance with his usual practice,
he sought the views of those present, beginning with the
most junior, myself. I said that it seemed doubtful whether
the Rhodesians really expected to reach agreement, on any

terms that we could publicly defend. If that were so, they would want their supporters to believe that the talks had failed because we, not they, were unreasonable. It would suit them for negotiations to break down on the question of Privy Council jurisdiction, partly because it was arcane and partly because it could seem inconsistent with genuine independence. It would be better for us to fudge, or broaden the points of disagreement, than to be boxed into that corner. The Prime Minister's political advisers, notably Gerald Kaufman, took a similar view. Jim Bottomley put the opposing one — that the Rhodesians *did* want an agreement and that we should not throw away the chance of getting one. By then it was time to meet the Rhodesian delegation and I sensed that the Prime Minister had made up his own mind against a settlement.

Given the shortage of time, and the conflicting advice he had received, I thought Wilson's handling of the final session was impressive. He did manage to broaden the discussion, I forget exactly how. The negotiations were suspended rather than terminated — though I think it must have been clear to most of us that the chances of an early settlement were now remote. I am fairly sure that it was clear to the Rhodesians. We heard from somebody who travelled on the same aeroplane that, on their return flight to Salisbury, they were as happy as sandboys; the strain was over and they could carry on as before.

My memories are vivid, but partial. I have not tried to complete them by a study of the papers; even if I had, the whole story would not necessarily emerge. But, as I see it (and saw it then), it would be wrong to suppose that an agreement was reached in *Fearless* that was later sabotaged. It would be truer to say that there was no agreement and no great expectation that the subsequent negotiations in Salisbury would succeed.

I did not go to Salisbury. George Thomson went, with Jim

Bottomley as his adviser. That left the deputy under-secretary, Sir Leslie Monson, as the official in London effectively in charge of Rhodesian matters. He had a Colonial Office background and a genuine concern for the advancement of the African majority; I believe that the attitude of the Smith regime, and of the white settlers who supported it, was personally distasteful to him. He was not a man to throw his weight about. But when the reports from Salisbury came through, I think he attended a high-level meeting, which either decided or recommended that George Thomson should not be given authority to settle on the terms available.

My role was confined to conferring with Monson and to doing some drafting. Late that evening, I took over a draft telegram to Number 10. As I was poring over it with one of the prime minister's secretaries, Wilson himself appeared, having just returned from a grand dinner. He stood in the doorway, in full evening dress and decorations, exuding wellbeing and good nature. I can recall his exact words: 'Very successful operation,' he said expansively, 'strong team there, strong team here.' Then he left. We sent off the telegram to Salisbury and so brought the negotiations to an end.

I could not help admiring the effrontery of the prime minister's assessment. If the *Fearless* operation had lessened the pressures on him, both from the right and from the left, well and good. From any other point of view, it had been a total failure. Or rather, it had been par for the course: we had limited the damage, but achieved nothing.

But, of course it was all part of a process — a process of gradually wearing down white Rhodesians' confidence in their ability to pursue policies that incurred world dis-approval. The process was repeated later in the partly similar case of South Africa.

In the autumn of 1969, when I left for The Hague, I

stopped worrying about Rhodesia. But two years of hard concentration on a single, if multi-faceted, problem had left its mark. I was in Algiers when, a decade later, I heard of the Lancaster House settlement. No foreign news has ever given me such a sense of relief. I felt sure that, whether or not Rhodesia would be better off without Britain, Britain would be better off without Rhodesia. It was clear to me, sitting in Algiers, that, whatever the future of Algeria, whatever personal tragedies had been and were involved, France had been right to withdraw.

8

Number Two

The Hague (1969–73)

E xcept for my two years in Washington, and about three of the years I spent in the Foreign Office, my diplomatic career was divided between the Middle East, Africa and western Europe. The western European part of it consisted of two postings to western European capitals (Paris and The Hague). It also included the year when I was an assistant in the Western Department. I was lucky to spend this year under Alan Campbell, a shrewd and kindly man, to whom I owed quite a bit both then and later.

A separate, and at that time more important, department handled Western organizations in the same corridor. So I was not directly concerned with the problems of NATO or of the European Community. German questions, such as the imprisonment of Hess and offset for the cost of British troops, took up most our time. But two very competent first secretaries handled them. I did pay a short working visit to Berlin, saw the wall and crossed into the old Wilhelmstrasse. The bulk of my time, however, was spent on France and Italy. We had a visit from the Italian prime minister and we had to arrange disaster relief for Venice. A senior official in the Treasury actually rang me up to suggest that we should not be too diffident in applying for funds. I wonder how many people have had that experience.

Our relations with France posed the most central problem. In 1963, three years before I joined Western Department, de

Gaulle had vetoed our accession to 'the Six' (the countries then comprising the European Community). Inevitably, this had strained Anglo–French cordiality. Although we were, in a sense, the injured party, we did not want to make matters worse by excessive sulking. But, perhaps we had become resigned to a certain stiffness in cross-channel relations. At any rate, when George Brown became foreign secretary in August 1966, he was determined to change this and to see that the French and the British were friends. All of us (though perhaps some, including myself, more than others) sympathized with this objective. Apart from anything else, it seemed the key to our eventual admission by the Six. But it was easier to advocate an improvement in relations than to bring it about. It takes two to tango and there was a need for restraint as well as ardour. Speeches had to be drafted warmly, yet carefully. In fact, four years were to pass before we were invited to open negotiations for our accession. The enlarged community of nine only came into existence on 1 January 1973.

I had personally liked the idea of closer European cooperation since I was an undergraduate. This was a natural reaction in somebody who had had his life distorted, however bloodlessly, by the war. Gladwyn Jebb, then in charge of reconstruction at the Foreign Office, came down to Oxford to give a talk while I was there. If I remember right, he propounded the classic postwar view that we had to ride both horses, the Atlantic and the continental. I asked him whether he thought that we could indefinitely keep our balance between them — whether we would not, sooner or later, need to sit more firmly in one saddle than in the other. He looked at me with a coldish eye and said (in effect) that he did not see why we should not ride both horses. I felt I had asked a silly question. But of course I had not. Perhaps the main criticism of our postwar foreign policy is that we tried to do too much, too long.

When I entered the Foreign Office I expressed a preference for working on European cooperation, though I was not surprised to find myself at a desk where confrontation (with the Soviet Union) was the order of the day. My sense of belonging to Europe deepened when I was in Paris. Personally, I found that a European dimension enriched rather than diluted my English/British experience. Then, when we set seriously about disbanding our empire, I felt that Dean Acheson was right. Shorn of empire, we needed a new role. I believed that Britain could not for long be satisfied with the sort of position held by neutral European countries. We were islanders, with a need to expand and to find scope for energy and ambition beyond our shores. In the postwar world, the Commonwealth could not be expected to provide the sort of enlargement we needed. If we tried to form a close association with the USA — and were admitted to one — we would always find ourselves a junior partner. So what was the alternative to Europe? After all, Britain was, and had always been, a part of Europe. For about three centuries England and Wales were in the Roman Empire. Our Norman kings held vast properties in France. There was once an English pope. Our culture (though much Americanized) was basically European. Our closest neighbours were European countries.

The economic advantages of closer European union were much debated then and are still debated now. Perhaps, at that time, there was too much assumption that big was beautiful. But, it seemed that British business needed the security and scope that only a common European market could reliably supply. Moreover, when European union gradually became a reality, contrary to the initial expectations of those who determined British policy towards it, there was the additional incentive that we would find ourselves odd men out, if we did not join — and could suffer accordingly.

We all know, or should know, that there is no perfection in government. No political system, no national or international bureaucracy will satisfy everybody or work flawlessly all the time. Over-centralization must tend to create discontent and set up resistance. But this is an argument for a reasonable degree of flexibility in practice. It is not an argument against attempts to create a European system capable of providing economic and other opportunities and designed to keep national conflicts within bounds.

I am myself less worried than many people are by the fear of having to surrender some pieces of national sovereignty. To put it crudely, I would sooner share them deliberately with allied governments than have to abandon them to financial or commercial pressures. Equally, it does not seem to me vital that *all* decisions, in external as well as in internal matters, should be arrived at democratically; I mind more about what decisions are taken than who takes them. What does seem to me important is that a country, like an individual, should have some long-term objective, which can give it hope and stimulate its energies. Of course, it can have internal as well as external objectives. But, in this country, we depend too much on the world outside to concentrate entirely and forever on our own internal concerns. We need an external role, as Dean Acheson implied; we need a direction for our foreign policy. It does not have to be exclusive, but we are not big enough to do everything well. When choices must be made, something has to come first.

As a nation, we have so far failed to make up our minds where the next phase of our international destiny lies. When we *have* made a decision, we have continued to call it in question. We are confused about what we can hope to achieve abroad. We accept that we are no longer a great power, in the way that we once were; but we think, rightly, that we still have considerable strengths. They are not

146

enough, however, to enable us to stand singly on our own high ground and tell the rest of the world what they ought to do.

The choice facing us is still fundamentally what it was 30 years ago. We have important interests — economic, military, cultural, diplomatic and historical — both in Europe and outside it. Which are we to put first? One role for Britain, which many people now seem to favour, would be that of a second-class — though still influential — global power. It would rely on American protection yet otherwise assert its independence; it would trade with the continent without being governed by Brussels; it would try to exploit the worldwide links bequeathed by its imperial past. No doubt this prospect has its attractions. But it raises questions that are not easy to answer. How will our international status be affected by the long-term consequences of devolution? Will Scotland and Wales want to go the same way as England? What will the dispositions be of a less and less waspish USA? How far will we be able to benefit from the advantages of European Community membership if we take such a restricted and self-centred view of our commitment to it? If the single currency proves a success, will we not want to join it? If it proves a failure (perhaps partly through our fault), will we not be faced by a disturbed and divided continent? If so, will we not find — as we have found so often in the past — that we are too close to our neighbours to detach ourselves from their problems?

The other main role open to us is that of a leading European power, fully committed to partnership with continental countries, maintaining outside interests but putting our European objectives first. Were we fully to accept that position, we could hope to use our influence to broaden the outlook of the Community and to prevent excessive centralization. Of course, there would be recurrent disappointments. But, if we can begin to think in terms of 'us' rather than 'them', it should not be beyond our powers to help shape the sort of community in which we can feel comfortable. By concentrating our energies and abilities on this aim, we could create a role for the future as challenging as the empire provided in its day. For all the optimism now felt in some quarters about the prospect of a 'global' role for Britain, it could only be the shadow of what we achieved in the eighteenth and nineteenth centuries. To escape — or at least to limit — post-imperial decline, we need to turn our thoughts in a new way.

Thirty years ago, when I was in The Hague, we did not anticipate that Euro-scepticism would become as vocal as it has recently been. My recollection is that most opinion-formers then were keen to overcome de Gaulle's veto and to join the European Community. At any rate, the question of our accession dominated my time at The Hague. It was the central objective of British foreign policy in those years and was bound to be the embassy's main preoccupation.

I arrived at The Hague after my rather gruelling spell as head of Rhodesia Political Department. I found that, although the atmosphere in the embassy was more peaceful, I was still quite fully occupied. I was number two and had to learn as much as I could about the place before the ambassador, Sir Peter Garran, retired at the end of 1969. The embassy staff had been cut quite recently; so I was head of Chancery as well as counsellor. The only other diplomat in the Chancery was a young third secretary, who was as new as I was.

I had not had much time to settle in when, on 1 and 2 December, the Six met at The Hague and, subject to the treaties of Rome, decided on the completion, strengthening and enlargement of the community. It was this meeting that paved the way for our accession, together with that of Ireland and Denmark (Norway of course withdrew after a referendum).

In the embassy, we could not hope to influence this meeting except by the representations we had already made to the Dutch. But we had to report its outcome, late at night, in order that the Foreign Office and British ministers could welcome it, or otherwise, early the following day. We had arranged for a Ministry of Agriculture official to join us from Brussels, so that he could find out from colleagues in the Six or the commission how things had gone. I had been asked to dinner by a Belgian diplomat and hoped to discover something there. I arrived late and left early, but was given to understand that we had more or less got what we wanted. Then I sat in the embassy, waiting for more precise information; a cypher clerk was standing by upstairs, ready to dispatch telegrams to London. An hour or so passed. The ambassador came in, but there was still no sign of the Ministry of Agriculture official. Finally, we tracked him down and he came in to report. I was (I think justifiably) rather terse; he took it quite well and, in due course, we had what was needed. It enabled us to telegraph, not only the broad gist but also quite a lot of the small print. Next morning, John Robinson, who as head of the European Integration Department held a key position throughout these negotiations, telephoned with his thanks.

In the following months, I had several contacts with the Dutch officials chiefly concerned with Community matters in the Foreign Ministry. They were all well known to John Robinson and were always helpful and accessible. I told them — and I believed it — that Britain's accession would strengthen the community, that — once the die had been cast — we would bring with us an aptitude for teamwork and an instinct for loyalty. (I remember these assurances a bit sadly now, though at the working level they have often been justified.) The Dutch were willing enough to hear such promises; but of course that was compatible with hard bargaining when their own interests were concerned. As I recall it, our main failure was over fish; the Foreign Ministry could not always control their fishery colleagues. One Friday afternoon (I cannot now remember exactly when) John Robinson rang up again. There was to be a meeting of the fisheries ministers of the Six, early the following week, in some other capital, when decisions were expected that could vitally affect our application to join the European Community. I might find it difficult to believe, he said, but this was more important than any other business there could possibly be on my desk. I was to drop everything, make an immediate appointment to see my regular contact at the Foreign Ministry, and put our case to him.

Although I was busy with other things, I of course accepted this and did as I was told. As usual, I had sympathetic hearing. I was assured (in effect) that the Dutch valued our accession too much to allow their Fisheries minister to jeopardize it. I went back to the office and sent reasonably optimistic telegram. There followed a long weekend, since Monday was a public holiday. On Tuesday morning, I read something in the Dutch press that made me wonder if all had gone well. Later, it became clear that the fisheries minister had kicked over Foreign Ministry restraints. We had no instructions from London, so I did not raise the matter again with my Dutch contact. But I thought he looked a little sheepish when I next called on him.

The new ambassador, Sir Edward Tomkins, thought the Chancery understaffed, which indeed it was, given the need for regular contact with the Dutch over our accession. He arranged for the head of Chancery post to be restored and for Juliet Collings (later mistress of Girton) to fill it as a first secretary, combining the job with a special brief for community matters. After her arrival, I spent less time on these myself — regretfully, since it had been the most interesting part of my work.

For the only time in my career, I became the interna

ffairs expert of the embassy. I rather enjoyed Dutch politics – a number of different parties reflecting different religious eliefs and social attitudes temporarily grouped in, or gainst, shifting coalitions. When a government falls in the Netherlands, a long period is usually required before a new ne comes into being. The queen appoints an *informateur*, vho finds out what sort of coalition might command ufficient support. Then there has to be a *formateur* who ctually composes the coalition. During the *interregnum*, fficials carry on the government without too much dif- iculty, provided there are no crises requiring a change of lirection. It is all very unlike the system we have been used o in this country. It makes for moderation, but not for lecisiveness.

I liked going to party conferences from time to time, ccompanied by Max Schuchart, a Dutch member of the mbassy staff, who gave me a lot of help. I could understand nost of the speeches because I had spent quite a lot of time earning Dutch. I was ashamed that, after 20 years in the ervice, I could only speak one foreign language fluently — rench. So I made an effort. I went for a week or two to a anguage laboratory in the south. I spent another week or wo with a Dutch family near Emmen. I had weekly lessons n The Hague. I listened to Dutch radio, read some Dutch lassics and took in Dutch newspapers.

Being able to read Dutch (and to understand it when well poken) turned out to be a great help to me in my work. It ook me a long way towards understanding the country. But never made much progress in speaking it, because my Dutch friends always wanted to practise, or show off, their nglish. This was not surprising, since their English was nuch better than my Dutch. It was, nevertheless, frustrating. once walked out of a restaurant because a waiter insisted n replying in English and said I had no need to pick up Dutch. I felt that, since I would be paying for my meal, this was for me to decide. In fact, many less-well-educated Netherlanders have no, or little, English; but most of my contacts belonged to the highly educated elite. I only remember two occasions when, for professional purposes, I needed to use my spoken Dutch. One was when the ambassador invited some trade unionists to the residence — they spoke excellent English, but not their wives. Another was when I called on two officials in the Ministry of Economic Affairs, who either had no English or were too shy to use it.

Perhaps there is no country in the world where there is more liking for the British people than the Netherlands. As a British diplomat, one senses this, almost on arrival. It is an advantage much envied by other diplomats. When I first met the German counsellor, she remarked on it, rather wistfully. There are racial, historical and religious reasons for this feeling of affinity between the Dutch and British. There was of course some hostility in the seventeenth century, when there were naval wars, and the British first used abusive terms like 'Dutch courage', 'Dutch uncles' and 'Dutch treats'. But since then, there has been much more neighbourliness than conflict. We never occupied the country, as the French did under Napoleon and the Germans during the war. Shell and Unilever are outstandingly successful international companies. Dutchmen usually prefer English to other foreign languages; they like to point out the words that are common to English and Dutch.

Of course, this does not mean that the Dutch are unaware of British faults or that they always approve of our policies. During my time in The Hague, Queen Juliana paid a state visit to London. The ambassador was in her suite, so I kept shop. I had looked forward, a bit sentimentally, to a celebration of Anglo–Dutch friendship. Instead, the Dutch press chose to represent their queen as an unhappy victim of English formality and condescension, getting a cool welcome from our own Queen and being rushed from ceremony to ceremony. As far as I could judge, the visit had been entirely successful — as such visits almost always are — and the accounts of any coolness were sheer invention. Certainly, Queen Juliana showed no sign of any resentment when I met her at the airport on her return.

There were two other occasions when I had evidence that even the best and easiest relationships need tact and care. A senior Foreign Ministry official who dealt with NATO said that he would like to have a talk. I asked him to lunch at my house. He spoke frankly, though in general terms, and told me that some Dutch feathers had been ruffled by arrogant, or seemingly arrogant, attitudes adopted by British naval spokesmen in dealing with their Dutch colleagues. Of course, I took note and passed this on.

There was also a naval aspect to the second occasion. One Friday afternoon, the Foreign Ministry rang up. When they found that the ambassador was not available (he was at a shoot, miles away, given by an important Dutch business-man), they summoned me to an immediate meeting with the Dutch foreign minister, Joseph Luns. It seemed that he was displeased with us. I just had time to brief myself rapidly on possible areas of difficulty; then I drove round. I found the minister alone, except for the political director of the ministry; he (Luns) was in a bad mood, having apparently attended a rather stormy cabinet meeting earlier in the day. He launched almost immediately into a complaint about British failure to cooperate; he had a failure in naval part-nership particularly in mind. At one point he referred to Britain, disparagingly, as 'an insular nation'.

I waited until he had finished and then asked if I might speak. I said what I could to justify the particular cause of grievance that he had raised. I went on to suggest that it was difficult to represent the Dutch as losers in their relations with us when, apart from anything else, the balance of trade was in their favour. Having let off steam, Luns had no wish

to go on arguing. He saw me out very civilly and wa
pleased to hear that I was learning Dutch; I thought that
though he might initially have spoken less roughly to th
ambassador, he was readier (because I was younger) to le
me have the last word once he had made his point. He was
commanding figure, with an international reputation uniqu
among Dutch foreign ministers. When he became secretar
general of NATO, in 1971, we recommended that he shoul
be given a high British decoration. I think it was on his las
day in the Foreign Ministry that the ambassador was able t
tell him that the Queen wished to make him a Companio
of Honour.

Dutch social legislation often attracted notice and interes
in Britain. They had a two-tier system of health treatment –
private insurance for the well-off and free care for the poor
They also had a rather different attitude towards strikes an
drugs — though the latter loomed less large than they d
today. It was not easy to find time to become expert in thes
matters, though I did learn a little. Sir Keith Joseph, the
secretary of state for social services, once came over for th
day. One evening, somebody at Number 10 rang up th
embassy; the Prime Minister, Edward Heath, wanted som
information about Dutch social practice (I cannot remembe
what). I could not be contacted; but the duty officer, wh
took the message, said that he could hear the Prime Ministe
himself walking impatiently up and down. I would not hav
been able to answer the question reliably if I had been there
I did my best next day.

Few peoples have more right than the Dutch to prid
themselves on democracy. They manage to combine a bia
towards conservative respectability with a remarkable degre
of liberalism. (I never quite got used to long-haired soldiers.
These trends go back a long way in their history, as doe
their philanthropy and their treasuring of individual rights
It does not follow that Dutch society, any more tha

American, is classless. The royal family may have behaved more informally than ours did at that time, but I do not think it was less exclusive or more accessible; on the contrary, it was allowed more privacy. The same might be said of the Dutch upper classes in general. There are seriously wealthy people in the Netherlands, though they hide their wealth more often than they display it. The gulf between the more and less educated cannot be much narrower than in Britain — in some cases it may be wider because Dutch university education lasts longer.

Except for a restaurant in The Hague, there is no House of Lords in Holland. There are no dukes or ducal estates. There are, nevertheless, little red books, which list members of the nobility, and little green books, which list members of the patrician class. Many of the latter descend from the upper middle class *regenten* of the seventeenth century. This was the fourth of the five classes into which Sir William Temple, ambassador at The Hague for a part of the reign of Charles II, divided Dutch society. He distinguished, first, the Clowns or Boors' (the peasants), plain, honest, diligent, but not very bright. Second, came 'the Mariners or Schippers', a much rougher set of people. Then there were the Merchants or Traders, who fill their towns'; these were more mercurial, very hard-working, quick to take advantage of others, but 'the plainest and best dealers in the world' when 'under the reach of Justice and Laws'. Above them, were 'the Renteneers' (*rentiers*), like the third class in modesty of dress and behaviour, but better educated, so as to fit them for their public role as magistrates. Lastly, there were 'the Gentlemen and Officers of their Armies'. Temple noted that there were few people of noble birth in the province of Holland, 'most of the families having been extinguished in the long wars with Spain'. He thought that such as survived tended to imitate the French too much, but were honest, good-natured and gentlemanly.

This was a simplified analysis; but it has not entirely lost its point today, in spite of the vast changes in Dutch society and economy since the golden century. The Netherlands still preserves patrician characteristics — even, though less obviously, some aristocratic ones. There are two clubs in The Hague that resemble their counterparts in Pall Mall — the Haagsche Club and the De Witte, the former being the more exclusive. I never went into either. When I arrived in The Hague the then ambassador, Sir Peter Garran, offered to get me into the Haagsche Club. I asked for a little time to think about it (I was afraid of falling into a particular social slot); he was a little surprised and I knew that the offer would not be renewed. Perhaps, I should have accepted it gratefully; but I doubt whether I would have used the club much, or whether membership would have made any difference to my work.

Peter Garran was an Australian of the old, very British school. He was impressed to hear that I had been friendly with Prince Claus, when he was Claus von Amsberg and number two of the German embassy in Abidjan. He said rather sadly that, in the old days, this would have been a great professional advantage, but he supposed that it would not count for much now. Von Amsberg's engagement was not at first popular in the Netherlands. I had written from Washington to congratulate him and to say that this would pass. He had replied that I should try to follow his example (I think he meant getting married, not necessarily to a princess). He had also invited me to come and see them when I was in Holland. So, I asked a private secretary to convey a message and, not long afterwards, the Prince did give me lunch in a restaurant in The Hague. He seemed genuinely pleased to meet a colleague from his diplomatic past and welcomed me warmly. It was more difficult to return his hospitality. A year or two must have passed before I was allowed to invite him to a small stag dinner party in my house; the only Dutch guest was the diplomat who used to polish his silver in Abidjan. It was a slightly stiff evening — I felt I had to call him 'Sir' — and I am not sure how much he enjoyed it, apart from the partridges, which he said his wife never gave him. Before I left the country I was bidden to lunch with him and Princess Beatrix (as she then was) at Drakesteyn, their charming country castle. It was very informal and they could not have been kinder. It did not occur to me to try to discuss politics or foreign affairs with them.

Not long before my appointment to The Hague a former Spanish ambassador there, the Duke of Baena, had published a book called *The Dutch Puzzle*, which caused a bit of a stir. There was a feeling in some Dutch quarters that, in what he had written about their royal family, he had abused his friendship with the Queen. It was, all the same, an intelligent and entertaining book. Through it, I first became interested in Sir William Temple, to the point of writing a book about him a few years later. I was struck by the elegance of a passage from Temple's *Observations upon the United Provinces*, which the Duke quoted:

> To conclude this Chapter: Holland is a Countrey where the Earth is better than the Air, and Profit more in request than Honour; where there is more Sense than Wit; More good Nature than good Humour; And more Wealth than Pleasure; Where a man would chuse rather to travel, than to Live; Shall find more things to observe than desire; And more persons to esteem than to love.

Again, this is a simplification, no doubt an oversimplification. But, again, it has not entirely lost its point.

I enjoyed the company of the sort of Dutch people I met in The Hague. Their mixture of principle and worldliness

reminded me of established professional families in Britain,
cultivated but not affected, restrained but not austere. Of
course, the atmosphere of The Hague is not necessarily
typical of the Netherlands as a whole. Like Washington, it is
a government city, flavoured by official values and modes of
behaviour, dependent first on the counts of Holland and
later on the House of Orange, enriched by the East Indies
rather than by modern industry. It is *deftig*, dignified or
'posh', in a way that other Dutch cities do not aspire to be.
It is also not as handsome as the best of them, except for the
area around the Mauritshuis. When I could, I used to spend
my Friday or Saturday evenings in Amsterdam, partly
because it was more stimulating and partly for the sheer
pleasure of walking along the canals. The distances are so
short and the roads are so good; I think it took me about
forty minutes to drive there.

There was a programme on Dutch television, called
(untranslatably) the *Fabeltjeskrant*, which I watched now
and again. It was played by animal puppets and was meant
for children; but it was also deservedly popular with adults.
I can only recall now three of the characters: the owl, the
beaver and the stork. The owl was, of course, wise; the
beaver spoke like a working man from Rotterdam; the stork
was a formidable *grande dame* with a posh Hague accent.
She pronounced the diphthong 'ei' quite differently from, for
instance, the beaver. I found all Dutch diphthongs difficult
enough to pronounce, without this additional complication.

Wassenaar, on the outskirts of The Hague, is a wooded
and wealthy (though not *ostentatiously* wealthy) suburb.
The counsellors of the embassy had had a biggish, oldish
house there; but my predecessor's Italian wife did not like it
and it had been taken over by the naval attaché. I had three
different addresses in The Hague. The place I liked most was
an old house near the centre; I only moved from it because,
as in Washington, my landlady wanted to sell it. It was not a

large house and the third secretary already occupied one floor; but it had charm and character and was in easy walking distance of the Chancery. I had a conscientious and efficient Portuguese maid who had two small children and came in on weekdays; an older woman used to cook for my dinner parties.

I spent nearly four years in The Hague, the longest posting in my career. I had chosen to go there — it was the only time when I was given an opportunity to say where I would like to go. It was rather a strain serving three different ambassadors — I was over 45 and becoming less adaptable — especially the third, who had exceptional gifts but a justified reputation for being difficult. In spite of that, I liked the country and enjoyed the greater part of my work. I felt that I had got on well with the people and learned something about them. When the time came, I wanted to end my career there. The personnel department agreed that it was a post that could be held by an unmarried ambassador; they offered the board a choice between another candidate and myself. To my great disappointment (and apparently after quite a long discussion) the other candidate was preferred.

That was at the end of 1980. In the summer of 1973 I left The Hague for Cairo, without much thought as to whether I might, or might not, come back.

* * *

Cairo (1973–75)

I arrived in Cairo in August 1973, more than twenty years after my drive to Baghdad in the Nairn bus. I had again crossed the Mediterranean by sea from Genoa; but this time I was driving my own car. I was, of course, older (getting on for 50) and higher in rank. I had been a counsellor for six years. Having been number two at The Hague, I was now to be number two at Cairo, a larger embassy.

The appointment was quite sudden. I thought I had lost touch with the Arab world and was hoping for a sabbatical year during which I could write a book. (I wanted a break of some kind and was ready to finance myself, for a short period.) The Foreign Office only asked me to go to Cairo when the appointment there of an Arabist fell through. I had never tried to get out of a posting; in any case, I was rather intrigued by this one. So, in spite of my hopes of a break, I accepted with more alacrity than the head of the personnel department had expected.

One of the reasons why I was intrigued was that, about thirty years earlier, I had sailed through the Suez Canal in LST 368 on our way to the Indian Ocean and the war with Japan. We had stopped in Port Said for a few days and of course had gone ashore there. There was a sort of cheap glossiness about the place, which was rather exhilarating; there were exciting smells; after the blackout at home it seemed a blaze of light. Another young officer and I managed a trip to Cairo. We saw the citadel and the museum as well as the pyramids from a distance. We also had lunch and cold lager in the crowded luxury of Shepherds' Hotel. I was trying to grow the first of my two beards (in the navy one had to be clean-shaven or stop shaving altogether). It was sprouting rather patchily and I remember buying a bottle of coconut oil from an Egyptian pharmacist. It did nothing to make my beard grow.

That was the only time I had landed in Egypt before 1973. I was not surprised to find it drabber and more claustrophobic than I remembered. The traffic too, must have greatly increased. Even now in England, when I hear more hooting than usual through my open window, I feel that I am in Cairo again.

Of course, as well as its dust, squalor and crowds, Cairo has the wide river and some places of beauty and quiet. The mosques far eclipse those of Baghdad. My own house was a bit above my station, in that the number two of the embassy used to be of minister's rank. A pleasant white house with blue shutters, the British Ministry of Works had built it, together with a few others in the same neighbourhood, shortly before the First World War. The neighbourhood was the island of Zamalek, which must have been at that time expensively suburban, if not rural. It had gone downhill, with overmuch building, but parts of it could still smell delicious in spring. We (the embassy) were much envied these Zamalek houses. My own had a garage and a square, medium-sized garden with datura blossoms and visiting hoopoes. In The Hague I had had one Portuguese maid who came in on weekdays. Here I had inherited a cook, a senior *suffragi* (butler), a junior one and a teenage gardener, besides a part-time washerwoman and a very dignified man who came once a week to press and sponge my clothes.

Cairo is not as hot as Baghdad in summer; but it is still hot. I slept sweatily in my bedroom, under a single sheet for fear of chills, with fixed nets across the open windows. In winter it could be quite cold in the evenings and it was comforting to burn fires. On some winter days, when the sun was up, the weather could be as glorious and stimulating as any I have come across. Of course, there were flies in the ointment, too — more or less literally. I never developed immunity to pinworm and tummy bugs. If I went into my kitchen in the evenings, I waited a minute after turning on the light; this was to give the cockroaches time to conceal themselves.

One should not generalize too much about national characteristics — or at least one should not exaggerate them. But the Egyptians speak softer Arabic than the Iraqis and, by and large, have softer manners. Perhaps when they are friendly, it means less than it would in an Iraqi. I have not been anywhere else where a smile tends to provoke such an instant and beaming response. There is electricity in an

Egyptian grin, which is difficult to resist; there is also a quickness to express feelings, which is sometimes disconcerting to inhibited foreigners. One fine holiday, I walked down a bank of the Nile to visit a mosque. I passed three youngish Egyptians sitting outside a café, drinking coffee. The oldest and plumpest of them called out to me 'Sir, you are beautiful.' This was an engaging but unexpected compliment. I was nearly 50 and I think his English must have been more flowery than my appearance.

British power had been felt longer in Egypt than in Iraq, though the period of direct peacetime administration was more remote. There was the same ambivalence in attitudes towards Britain and the British. But there had been many changes in the Middle East between 1953 and 1973; after Nasser, no sane Egyptian could really suppose that we were governing the country behind the scenes. Yet, under the surface, there was still a certain prickliness and readiness to take offence, which any hint of colonial bossiness could easily revive. I was once talking to a wealthy, but radically minded Egyptian (younger than myself), who enjoyed Western society. Somehow, the name of the famous proconsul, Cromer, cropped up. Cromer practically governed Egypt, as British agent and consul general, from 1883 to 1907. When he left the country, he drove through silent crowds to the station. He knew himself that he and his countrymen were not popular; but he hoped that the Egyptian fellaheen 'might remember with some feeling akin to gratitude that it was the Anglo-Saxon race that first delivered them from the thraldom of their oppressors'. I suggested to my friend that modern Egyptians ought not to portray Cromer as an ogre; according to his lights, he had worked hard for the welfare of the country. When I saw that this had not gone down well, I added that perhaps it was too early to be talking in these terms; my friend hastily agreed. Nationalists tend to have longer memories than imperialists.

As formerly in Baghdad, our embassy in Cairo is on the river bank. The ambassador's residence is suitably palatial; the Chancery offices are housed in a more modern building nearby. Cairo has traditionally been the main British post in the Arab world, except where oil is concerned. The embassy there is the pinnacle of an Arabist's career, unless he goes to the very top of the service. My ambassador, Sir Philip Adams, was an experienced Arabist who had a very good touch with the Egyptians. Both he and his wife were popular with the staff and were more than kind to me personally. Most educated Egyptians speak English and the ambassador was quite content that I should not be an Arabic speaker. It remained the case that I was a non-Arabist, surrounded by Arabists and taking over from one.

Because of that I never felt as essential a part of the embassy as I had at The Hague. Besides, I was getting older and was looking for promotion. So, though I quite enjoyed my time in Cairo, I found it less satisfying than most of my service abroad. I did have one longish spell in charge of the embassy when the ambassador was on leave. If there were any political crises during that time, I have forgotten them. I remember putting up Sir Hugh and Lady Wontner, when he was paying an official visit as Lord Mayor. They were taken on a sweltering tour of the pyramids; but we managed to have one relaxed evening. I also gave lunch to Jack Jones, then a great power in the trade union world and much courted by the media. He, too, was on an official visit. I was relieved to find that he had no anti-Palestinian bias. But he seemed implacable on European union and put me firmly in my place when I ventured to suggest that British business needed to know where it stood.

I arrived in Cairo two months before the October war (what the Israelis call the Yom Kippur War). Israel had been in hot or cold conflict with its Arab neighbours throughout the 25 years of its existence. In 1956, at the time of the Suez crisis, its forces had reached the Canal; in 1967 they had defeated Egypt, Syria and Jordan in six days, capturing the whole of Sinai, the Golan Heights, east Jerusalem and the West Bank. In October 1973, the Egyptians and the Syrians managed to hit back. Almost nobody had been expecting this. When I got to Cairo, the atmosphere of secrecy surrounding the government was almost palpable. Not surprisingly, President Sadat involved as few people as possible in the development of his policies. The well-known journalist, Heikal, sometimes provided indications of the regime's intentions; diplomats scrutinized his articles as carefully as any Delphic oracle. But to find an Egyptian who really knew what was happening, and was prepared to talk about it, was virtually impossible. Diplomats carefully treasured their few contacts, however unreliable, and were reluctant to share them with their colleagues. I did pay some initial calls on Egyptian officials who had had dealings with my predecessor. One of them, who worked for Sadat's son-in-law, gave me a clue that I think I should have taken more seriously. When I said something to the effect that his government seemed to have opted for patience in their Israeli policies, he looked unhappy. He mumbled that they could not be expected to put up with Israel's occupation of Egyptian territory. I took this as an aspiration, not as any indication of a plan.

I never got closer to Sadat than a handshake; but the ambassador had two or three night-time conversations with him during the war. I have always felt that he had much in common with the French emperor, Louis Napoleon: both men of flexible and imaginative minds, both with the instincts of statesmen, both with the habits of conspirators. Until the start of the war, foreign diplomats in Cairo had more or less unanimously decided that we were all in for 'a long haul'; Sadat was thought to have concluded that, for the time being, there was nothing he could do to improve the Egyptian position *vis-à-vis* the Israelis. At first I may have been inclined to question this analysis; but by October I had come to assume that it was probably correct.

So, when war broke out, it came as a startling surprise, to me as to everybody else. The head of Chancery in our embassy, who had previously argued the 'long haul' thesis, was quicker than I to accept the evidence that it had been wrong. Very soon, there was no room for doubt. We had a summons from the Ministry of Foreign Affairs. The ambassador was in Alexandria that weekend (of course he came back as soon as he could); so I had to go to the ministry to be formally notified that the Egyptians had crossed the canal into Sinai. I was careful to avoid any expression of approval or disapproval. I asked one or two questions and sent a telegram to the Foreign Office drafted so as not to raise any unnecessary hackles.

Our concern, of course, was that there should not be some initial reaction in London, which would condemn the crossing, either explicitly or implicitly. If there had been, it would have been difficult for us to shake off the appearance of being anti-Arab, whatever the progress or outcome of the war. This was well understood in the Foreign Office, too; but I think our reporting and advice were a help to them. At any rate, when the crisis was over, we had a message of appreciation from Tony (later Sir Anthony) Parsons. I had known him years before when he was assistant military attaché in Baghdad, and had lunched with him before coming out to Cairo; the message he left with me was a simple one: good relations with Egypt were vital, at least until we could supply our own oil needs. Ministers accepted this advice during the October war. From the Arab point of view, we did not do quite as well as the French, whose foreign minister said that somebody could hardly be criticized for returning '*chez soi*'. But we behaved as well as, perhaps better than, they expected.

At the beginning of the war, the atmosphere in Cairo wa excited and a bit apprehensive. Attempts at blackou reminded me of wartime Britain though, since there had been no time to organize civil defence, they were not very thorough. Not long after the crossing, I drove out, through unusually empty streets, to the pyramids, where I used to ride. The sounds of gunfire could be heard quite distinctly During most of the war, however, we kept to our offices and our homes. The secrecy that had shrouded the preparations for war continued to shroud its progress. But, of course telegrams were repeated to us from all round the world Simply to read and digest them was a full-time job; it was also an absorbing one. Our other main source of inform ation was the world service of the BBC; anyone unfamiliar with the tune of 'Lillibullero' got to know it now. It was rather as if we were spectators of a particularly enthralling football match; like other football spectators, we found our-selves becoming partisan and emotionally involved. We supported the Egyptian side because we were living in Egypt, because we were Arabists or Arabophile and because we were sincerely pleased that the supposedly (and too often actually) inefficient Arabs had managed to pull off a remarkable coup.

The initial reaction was overly euphoric. The crossing at first suggested that the Egyptians would feel a totally new confidence in themselves and that the balance of power in the region would be completely altered. Later, it became clear that, after the first surprise had been achieved, the Israelis had rallied and the Egyptians had not been able to sustain their advance. Some time after the fighting had stopped, I met an affable Egyptian general at a drinks party in a houseboat on the Nile. He spoke with great earnestness about the horrors of modern warfare, as if the struggle had almost been beyond human strength to pursue or endure. Nevertheless, when the smoke lifted, it was clear that much had changed. The Arabs did have more confidence. Unfortunately for the West, this encouraged a solidarity that led to the oil crisis. I am not sure now that we ever knew at all definitely what role the Egyptians played in promoting concerted action by the Arab oil producers, though I think I remember them listening politely when we put the case against. It was as political and military leaders, not as oil producers, that they were important in Arab strategy. They were also well placed to influence the Arab League, which then had its offices in Cairo.

One striking development in Egyptian polices after the war was the great improvement in their relations with the USA. At the time of the crossing, the chief American representative in Cairo was a youngish man of, I suppose, first secretary rank. I think that both he and we expected that he would be in for a difficult time, because of his country's close ties with Israel. In fact, it was the reverse that happened. When Sadat realized that he was not going to achieve a clear-cut victory, he seems to have decided that it was only through Washington that he could bring pressure to bear on the Israelis. So the Americans began to be courted in Cairo, not execrated. Dr Kissinger began his celebrated shuttle diplomacy. There was a move towards greater economic liberation. Private enterprise produced a few early blossoms.

I have never set foot on the Sinai peninsula. But, some time after the war, the Egyptian foreign ministry organized a coach trip to Suez for heads of mission in Cairo. Since the ambassador was away, I took his place, sitting next to the Italian ambassador. There was plenty of rubble to see and some signs of restoration; when we got to Port Tewfik, I had difficulty envisaging the sprucely elegant French Club where I had had a gin and tonic as an RNVR midshipman 30 years earlier. But the main drama of the outing was an accident to our coach. At one point it skidded on a desert road, did a neat U-turn into the sand and then collapsed — with slow dignity — on its side. Nobody was seriously hurt. I was comfortably cushioned by the Italian ambassador — or was it the other way round? In either case, we managed not to harm each other. When finally we escaped, we saw the driver sitting on the desert, covering his head with sand, and bemoaning his fate. The poor fellow was presumably contemplating early retirement and, with a proper sense of priorities, our Egyptian escorts were completely absorbed in consoling him. After an hour or so of diplomatic sang-froid, an Egyptian officer appeared with fresh transport. 'Dreadful sorry for the accident that has been happened' he said to us, beaming. We beamed, a little wanly, back.

After the war, the rest of my two years in Cairo was a bit of an anti-climax. For commercial as well as political reasons, we did what we could to ensure that Britain still counted for something. The Royal Navy proceeded to clear mines from the canal, with a view to its reopening. This involved me in lengthy negotiations with a lawyer at the Foreign Ministry, who sometimes behaved as if the Egyptians were doing us a favour rather than the other way round. I was stung into a brief display of bossiness, followed by contrition. In the end we worked out an agreement, which he regarded with some complacency. But, by then, the work (or most of it) had been done and I doubt if either side ever invoked the document.

Another agreement, for cultural cooperation, involved me in negotiations that were still lengthier but less fraught. The British Council was well represented in Cairo and formed an important part of the British presence there. There was a lot of work, too, over an Egyptian request that we should use development aid money to improve the baggage handling facilities at Cairo airport (they certainly needed improving). There was a reasonable feeling in London that this would not directly benefit the Egyptian peasants (Cromer's fella-

heen). We in Cairo took the view that the existing arrangements discouraged growth in travel and tourism that would
benefit the Egyptian economy as a whole. In any case, we
were under considerable pressure from the Egyptians and
were afraid that, if we refused, they would take it as a slap
in the face — the last thing that we wanted to give them in
the brave new world after their crossing of the canal. After
all, we had no money available for purely political gestures.
Eventually, we got our way; but the aid lobby in London
was not pleased.

From time to time, I would call on a Jordanian official of
the Arab League. We discussed Palestine, rather too optimis-
tically, in the changed circumstances of the Middle East. I
tried to convey a sympathetic attitude without being too
committal. In Britain then, there was less understanding of
the Palestinian viewpoint than there is now, more unre-
served support for Israel. Ever since before the Second
World War, left-wing critics had attacked pro-Arab bias in
the Foreign Office. In my time, quite apart from the rights
and wrongs, most Foreign Office officials regarded our
interests in the Arab world as crucial. They were nevertheless inhibited by fears of political repercussions from
risking too much offence to Israel. When we submitted from
Cairo a reasoned proposal for a British initiative on
Palestine, senior officials did not submit it to ministers. They
could gauge how it was likely to be received.

There was no separate oriental secretariat in Cairo, as
there had been in Baghdad. But more of my time was spent
on external matters, because the internal political situation
seemed relatively static and we no longer had any special
responsibility for Egyptian development. The squalor in
many parts of Iraq could be felt as a reproach. One got used
to it, as I had got used to beggars in India during the Second
World War; one said to oneself that squalor did not always
mean misery and that it was less dreadful to people who had

169

never known anything else. Of course, there was some truth in that and of course it would have done no good to be too distressed by what one could not help. All the same, it was difficult to avoid a feeling of uneasiness and a wish to help things improve. In Cairo, there was squalor on a larger scale and the pressures of overpopulation were immense. (Here again, there could be squalor without misery, though there was no doubt misery enough.) But, I do not remember ever feeling that this was my business, except in a very general sense. Equally, when I was posted to Algiers, the over-population and overcrowding was profoundly depressing, but not a reproach to me personally. It was beginning to be a matter of political concern, since it might seem to threaten the stability of the regime, but it was not a moral problem for the outsider. When I was in Cairo it was a socio-economic rather than a political problem. The stability of the regime seemed assured.

One result of relatively successful Egyptian military action, as well as of concerted measures by the oil producers, was the rather short-lived experiment of the Euro–Arab dialogue. In Cairo, I think we were sceptical about its prospects, except as a talking shop. My own experience in Baghdad had convinced me that economic aid and technical assistance were normally conducted more effectively on a bilateral than a multilateral basis. However, during the summer of 1975, the Foreign Office wished to create a new post of assistant undersecretary, in charge of the British contribution to the dialogue. I was due for promotion and had served in two European and two Arab countries, so I must have been a fairly obvious choice. They wrote to my ambassador about it; but, in the event (and to my relief when I heard about it), the post was not at that time created. My name was instead submitted for another undersecretary post, which I think might have suited me quite well, while an exact contemporary of mine was put forward for a further undersecretary post, as head of planning. In its wisdom, the board switched the two of us round. So, when I left Cairo in August 1975, two years after arriving there, it was as head of planning elect.

Before I left I managed to fit in a brief visit to Luxor, Aswan and Abu Simbel, though there was no time for a Nile cruise. Previously, I had seen very little of Egypt outside Cairo and its neighbourhood. The ambassador had at his disposal a flat in a British government property in Alexandria. He and his wife were kind enough to lend it to me once or twice at weekends. I found little to recall the city of the Ptolemies, or even the city of Cavafy; but the district around the ambassador's flat was pleasantly, if shabbily, evocative of the south of France. I did not do anything very exciting there. I had an idea for a book, which I wrote after my retirement; I bought some Bohemian glass in an antique shop; I spent an inordinate amount of time removing seeds from a loofah. What I most enjoyed was dining in an almost empty restaurant to the repeated strains of 'Onward Christian Soldiers'. I suppose that was a relic of British wartime occupation. Another such relic was the Anglo–Egyptian Friendship Bar in a seedy part of Cairo. One of my colleagues claimed to have gone in there, saying cheerily: 'Here's the Anglo half. Where's the Egyptian?'

On another weekend my car broke down in the desert; it overheated when I was trying to get to a hotel on the north coast. Somehow, I got back, carless, to Cairo. It was after dark and I had to burgle my way into my house because none of the servants lived in. I can still call to mind the fresh, sweet smell of the herbs in my garden as I trod on them.

This accident relieved me of my car; but, as in Baghdad, I had to dispose of my horse when I left Egypt. I had bought him from stables by the pyramids, where he was called Mish-Mish (Apricot, from his colour). Somebody told me that I could not possibly own a horse with such a common name; so I weakly renamed him Murad. I usually managed to ride him twice a week for an hour or so, on my own. Occasionally I had a companion; once a party of us rode to some ruins for the night and mosquitoes savaged us (but it was worth it). I had learned to ride as a boy in England, where I had been trained to break quietly into a trot from a walk and into a canter from a trot. The stables staff could not bear to see me trying to teach this cumbersome procedure to Murad, so I had to learn to go straight into a gallop, in the Arab fashion. This was exhilarating — all the more so because it had, for me, the charm of what was wicked and forbidden. In August 1975, I rode Murad for the last time and sold him back to the stables, where I suspect he promptly became Mish-Mish again. I have never had a horse of my own since.

9

Euro–Arab Dialogue

The Dialogue (1976–77)

Back in London I did not survive very long as head of planning. For one thing, I was never very comfortable in the job; I had always felt that machinery should be as simple as possible and that each Foreign Office department should do its own planning. For another, I had probably put some backs up, in spite of good advice to the contrary. Even if I had not, there was a case for downgrading the post, which had originally been held at head of department (counsellor) level. Not long after I returned, Michael Palliser took over as permanent undersecretary. He had been a successful planner himself as a counsellor; when I told him that I was not desperate to keep the job, he took me (a little too rapidly, I thought) at my word.

The temptation as a planner is to pursue objectives too single-mindedly. I had a staff of three bright first secretaries who, though realists, had developed a strong *esprit de corps*. Spurred by them, and by the example of my predecessor, I tried to behave with the logic and incorruptible detachment that seemed to be expected. We produced a paper on Africa (I advised people not to worry too much about the Soviet threat there); we proposed a European fishing conference; we were perhaps a little too consistent in our suggestions for disbanding the remains of the colonial empire. I ought to have obtained more support for some of these ideas, or not put them forward.

Whether or not there is a need for planners to interfere in particular areas of foreign policy, somebody in the Foreign Office has to cope with matters of general concern. There was some political demand for a paper on the principles of British foreign policy that could be made public. This was not an easy thing to produce; it was hard to steer between the sands of platitude and the rocks of contention. I inherited a draft, which was not very good. I improved it, but it was still unimpressive and the project was quietly dropped. I did write a confidential paper on what seemed to me the main foreign policy questions that needed to be tackled. I think it made some good points, but served little purpose; it was little discussed, though not wholly rejected. Quite a lot of our work also involved preparation for the possibility of devolution in the United Kingdom. Other government departments were of course more closely concerned; but there were implications for the conduct of foreign affairs.

I heard once or twice that the secretary of state (Jim Callaghan) wished to see me. Eventually, a time was fixed in his busy schedule. His concern was to impress on me how easily things could go wrong. He wanted me to keep an eye open and warn him at an early stage of possible danger around the world. I was not quite sure whether he really felt the need of my personal advice, or whether he simply wanted to know what I looked like, in case he should ever wish to consult me. Of course, I promised that I would do my best. On my way out I rather rashly said to his private secretary: 'The Secretary of State wants me to be the most important man in the Office.' I meant it as a joke — it was so patently not the case. I am not sure that it was taken as such.

One of the few things I remember with pleasure from this period was a visit to Tokyo to talk to the Japanese planners. The senior member of my staff (Thorold Masefield), who went with me, had organized it. In talking to the Japanese, enjoyed expatiating freely on world affairs without any risk of being held to account for what I said; I found it much easier than I expected. One evening, they gave us an expensive traditional dinner in an atmosphere of austere luxury. We were also able to admire Japanese tradition at Kyoto. We took a train there on the Saturday, together with a member of the embassy staff who was making arrangements for a visit by Callaghan. Then we broke our journey home at Peking, where I had more talks, less formally. This was the only time that I have ever been to the Far East.

When it was decided to downgrade my post I was not very happy to find that I was to be 'Mr Euro–Arab Dialogue' after all. It might be more or less a full time job when we held the presidency of the European Community; but it would certainly not be before or after. Given the speed with which my successor as head of planning had been selected, I felt a little cynical when I was asked at the last moment to stay on a bit longer. This was to enable me to coordinate a Foreign Office response to a new Whitehall enquiry into our procedures. In the previous few years, there had already been the Plowden and Duncan reports. It seemed to me that this further enquiry was bound to be a waste of time and money, especially since it was apparently concerned to impress opinion at home rather than to consider effects abroad. However, the powers that be decided to cooperate. I remember having one brush with Lady Blackstone (as she now is). When her team reported, I was no longer involved. But I never heard that much had been achieved by this exercise.

On my translation (if that is the right word), I had to exchange a convenient office on the ground floor, overlooking St James's Park, for a spacious but rather dingy attic. Instead of a portrait of Danby, Charles II's minister, I had one of an obscure maharajah. What was more upsetting was that, as I had expected, time fell heavily and I was seldom able to keep my personal assistant fully occupied. An active desk officer in the European Integration Department, who was more than capable of dealing with most matters that cropped up, did the routine work of the dialogue. I was busy enough before and during international meetings. In between I had little to do except write to other government departments or posts abroad when an undersecretary's signature was needed. Temperamentally, I am not inclined to invent work though, equally, I will try to cope with all of it that comes my way. As head of planning, I had perhaps tried to do too much; now I was obliged to do too little. Another frustration was that, since I had no department to supervise, I was supposed to conform to policies laid down by the European Integration chain of command. These were sometimes applied more rigidly than they need have been and, with more experience, I would have ignored them more confidently than I did. In fact, my position was rather that of a roving ambassador, acting on instructions though with the discretion that an ambassador must always have, rather than that of an undersecretary, helping to determine policy.

The practical work of the dialogue was divided between a number of committees, covering trade, investment, technology transfer and other possible areas of cooperation. Twice a year, the general commission was supposed to meet. At these meetings, senior European and Arab officials would confront each other and review the work of the committees; in advance of them each side would confer internally, so that concerted positions could be reached. When smaller Euro–Arab meetings were needed, at the senior official level, the 'troika' principle applied on the European side. (Under this principle, the representative of the country holding the presidency of the European Community conducts negotiations, with the support of his predecessor and successor in that position.) During my time, there were three meetings of the general commission: the first was at

Luxembourg in June 1976, the second at Tunis in February 1977 and the third at Brussels in October 1977. The UK held the presidency in the first half of 1977; so I was a member of the troika for most of my 18 months.

Other Whitehall departments tended to be still more suspicious of the dialogue than our posts abroad were. I called once on a senior Department of Trade official to appeal for more cooperation. At another time I wrote to a Treasury official to say that the Foreign Office was not 'starry-eyed' about the dialogue, but that we had to be able to display a modicum of goodwill. In order to show that we took the dialogue seriously we tried to give it some practical content. Even when there was a readiness to cooperate, we were never very successful in these efforts; but it was not only through the fault of the Europeans that in the end little or nothing of practical value was achieved. At the same time the dialogue was also an exercise in conciliation — trying to break down suspicion. As such, it may have been a little more successful. At the very least, it had to be handled as a 'damage limitation' exercise — and I think that any serious damage was in fact avoided.

The contacts we Europeans had with the Arabs might have been better, but could easily have been much worse. The contacts we British had with our European partners — and they with us and each other — seemed to me, on the whole, a model of political cooperation. Each country kept its freedom of action; but there was a genuine wish to cooperate, which usually produced good results. Of course, we were not dealing with really vital matters of national interest. We were friendly with each other personally and we all recognized that political cooperation of this kind offered considerable advantages to each of our countries. So long as we stuck together, the Arabs could not try to play us off against each other. We would not be forced to take part in a race for their favours.

As well as the first three meetings of the general commis
sion, I took part in preparatory European meetings a
Luxembourg and Lancaster House, troika meetings at Th
Hague and a small meeting with the Arab League in Cairc
before the Tunis general commission. In Tunis, I had to leac
the European side. By the time of the Brussels genera
commission I was preparing to go to Algiers and was nc
longer actively working on the dialogue in the Foreigi
Office. But I represented the UK at the Brussels meeting.

Perhaps I could have done more in London to make some
thing of the dialogue. But I did contribute something to th
three meetings of the general commission that I attended
Naturally enough, the Arabs wanted to use the dialogue tc
separate the European countries from Israel (and from th
USA as supporters of Israel) and to obtain their backing fo
Arab causes, particularly the creation of a Palestinian state
The attitudes of the European countries were not identica
but we all had firm instructions not to go too far. On th
last evening of the meeting at Luxembourg, the Arabs wer
upset that we had conceded so little on the political front
They were conferring among themselves. We (the Euro
peans) were sitting wearily, and somnolently, in anothe
room. From what we could judge, there was a real dange
that the Arabs would go away in a huff; but there appearec
to be nothing we could do about it. It seemed to me that
though the dialogue was unlikely to achieve any substantia
results, its breakdown might do some real harm. I though
we must hold out a small olive branch. I asked Davic
Blatherwick, an Arabist who was advising me, whether h
could think of a formula that would soften our positio
without going too far. He worked out a phrase in Arabic
which I persuaded my colleagues to back. We sent it roun
and, by good luck, it arrived in time; it became possible fo
the Arabs to reach agreement with us without losing face.

The whole business of diplomacy has become so collectiv

that it sometimes looks as if there is little scope for personal initiative at any level, whether ministerial or official. I was fully conscious that the proceedings at Luxembourg would not shake the world; but I could not help feeling a little excitement that my personal intervention had made a difference. My European colleagues were grateful for it and said so — particularly the Luxembourg delegation, who had worked hard to make the occasion a success. David Blatherwick's formula was regarded as a magic spell — all the more so because none of us could fully seize its significance in Arabic.

At Brussels, my intervention was behind the scenes and unauthorized by my European colleagues. I found the leading Arabs in distress because they thought they had been treated like schoolboys — a case of rigid instructions being applied a little too rigidly. The Arab League official I used to know in Cairo was among them (this did not stop him being as suspicious of me as of everybody else). I dare say they were so glum because they knew that they must keep their personal resentment to themselves; they did not want the meeting to break down any more than we did. But I may have helped to calm them; at any rate I pulled out all the stops I could.

At Tunis, of course, I had a more central role, since I was leading the European side. I was lodged in a spacious hotel suite and supplied with daily baskets of fresh fruit. The least I could do in return was to make my opening speech in the three official languages of the dialogue: French, English and Arabic. David Blatherwick had coached me in the Arabic section. He was never very satisfied with my pronunciation, but it must have been just intelligible because afterwards an Arab lady delegate addressed me in Arabic in the hotel lift. But my most challenging experience at Tunis was a troika meeting with the chief Arab delegates, at which I had to field political questions, particularly on Palestine. On the whole, I was satisfied with the way this went. My Belgian colleague told his wife afterwards that I had been 'brilliant'. David Blatherwick's assessment was more accurate. I had answered some questions better than others, but, generally speaking, it had not been too bad.

That was before I developed a nasty attack of influenza, which my French colleague attributed to sleeping under an open window. It was not helped by the sleepless last night of the meeting, when I had to make a final speech in the small hours. Before then I had appeared, croaking, on Tunisian television. Almost immediately after I got back to London, I was required to attend a meeting between David Owen, then minister of state at the Foreign Office, and some MPs. Diagnosing me rapidly from a safe distance, he said severely: 'You may not realize it, but you are highly infectious.' I do not know whether it was because of this, or because officials ought to be seen but not heard, that I was not asked to say anything at the meeting, though the dialogue was being discussed and I was the only person present who had been at Tunis.

Not long after the Tunis meeting my feet began to swell and, in due course, I was found to have kidney disease. My doctor thought that, though there must have been some latent propensity, it could have been 'triggered' by my influenza. I had been nominated ambassador at Algiers and there was some question whether I should go there; but it was eventually decided that I could. I was able to tell my Arab friends at Brussels about this appointment. They regarded Algiers as an important post (it was more important for them than it was for us) and congratulated me.

When I left the Brussels meeting I thought I had finished with the dialogue. I had no hard feelings about it, though it may have cost me my health; but enough seemed to be enough. However, after I got to Algiers, the Foreign Office had difficulty in finding somebody able or willing to lead the

British delegation at the next meeting of the general commission. They asked me to do so and to fly from Algiers for the preparatory meetings. I was new in my post and wanted to make a success of it; I had no political staff in Algiers and was not very well physically. So I opted out. I never heard of the dialogue again.

* * *

Algiers (1977–81)

I was told of my appointment to Algiers in the spring of 1977, during the rather unsatisfactory period when I had not got enough to do. I had complained that I was not being put to full use. The head of personnel said that the board had taken me at my word. I think he meant that relations with the Algerians were difficult and that I would have no political staff to support me. I did not mind too much about that. Algeria might not come high in the list of British priorities; but it was not an unimportant country. After three more or less challenging years there I hoped to end my career in a European capital.

This was before, though not long before, the discovery of my kidney disease. After that there was some discussion between my doctor and the Treasury doctors as to whether I could take up the appointment. In the end, it was arranged that I should return to London for a flying visit every few months to be medically tested. Later on, I was ordered to avoid protein; at this stage I was encouraged to eat a lot of it, to make up for what my kidneys were losing. Somebody warned me that my diet in Algiers might be deficient in protein. So I bought a vast cheese and several packets of Complan. In fact, when I got there, I found it was quite easy to get meat if, unlike the average Algerian, you could afford it. I never touched the Complan, though I did eventually finish the cheese.

I arrived in Algiers early that December, together with my private car, in a French ship from Marseilles. I was met by Brian Hitch, my number two, and by an Algerian protocol official, who apparently scolded one of the ship's officers quite severely for not having taken any special notice of me.

On my three previous visits to Algiers I would not have expected any French or Algerian authority to take notice of me. The first visit was in the spring of 1956, when I was at Paris. The Algerian war for independence had been smouldering, or burning, in the interior for about 18 months. Nobody seemed to know whether the French were winning or losing it; even the nomenclature of the parties was often a mystery. Jebb decided that our consulate general was too involved in routine dealings with the French authorities to be able to report authoritatively on what was happening and on the likely outcome. On the other hand, he had no wish to embarrass our relations with France by any high-level intervention. So I was sent out to discover what I could, as unobtrusively as possible — unobtrusively, but not secretly, since I would have to call on people able to give me reliable information. The consulate general arranged most of these interviews for me, but otherwise left me to my own devices. As well as Algiers, I visited Oran, Bône (now Annaba) and Constantine. I was armed with a questionnaire compiled by Anthony Meyer, who later became an MP and stood against Mrs Thatcher. At that time he was covering, brilliantly, French internal affairs.

I believe I was able to answer most of the detailed questions more or less adequately. I also wrote a general report on my return, which concluded that the French were on their way to losing control of events, that they would need to make a great effort to regain control and that, even after that, there was no obviously satisfactory long-term solution from their point of view. I might have put my conclusion still more starkly, if I had not been working at Paris and concerned about Anglo–French relations. Some time later, General de Gaulle was supposed to have returned from an Algerian visit saying of his compatriots there: '*Ils sont foutus.*' (This f-word, according to my dictionary, is not in decent use.)

At that time I might have enjoyed spending a holiday in the coastal strip of Algeria. The French/Spanish/Italians were still a long way from packing their bags. There were parts of Algiers where 'Arab' Algerians were hardly to be seen, except for cleaning ladies, shrouded in black. More than half of the taxi-drivers and waiters appeared to be of European stock. At the upper social levels almost everybody was. There were gleaming buildings, sophisticated bars and restaurants and well-kept vineyards. In all sorts of ways, the *oeuvre française* in Algeria was genuinely impressive. Its fatal weakness was that, at least in the coastal area, it was predominantly a work of Europeans for Europeans.

I was able to answer some detailed questions and make one or two general predictions. But I could not find out what was happening on the ground. We did not understand then the nature of guerrilla warfare as well as we do now — how relatively easy it is for small groups of organized and determined men, with a degree of popular support, to baffle larger groups of professional soldiers. I could not discover what was happening, because few, or no, people on either side really knew. It would not have been suitable for me to talk to rebels, even if I had been able to contact them. Nor had I any meetings with French soldiers; those (if any) who did know what was happening kept it to themselves. It was my first, but no means my last, experience of Algerian secrecy. Once, in a railway compartment, I was alone with an elderly Algerian who looked like a farmer. I tried to get him to talk a little, but he would not say anything. I dare say that, being fairly prosperous, he was a supporter of the status quo.

My second visit to Algiers was six years later. By that time foreigners were counting on Algerian independence; but General Salan's organization, the OAS, was carrying out terrorist attacks on those who advocated it. The richer *colons* were making plans to leave; the poorer *colons* were still hoping, if not always expecting, to stay. I was on my way to Abidjan by sea. My friend Christopher Ewart-Biggs (later to be assassinated as ambassador at Dublin) was in Algiers, preparing the ground for the embassy that we expected to set up before long. He and his wife Jane took me out to lunch in a restaurant. It was 16 March, a day after the OAS had carried out a particularly brutal attack on a social centre in El Biar. Not very many people were stirring in the streets; I have a vague memory of gunfire somewhere; otherwise our lunch was uninterrupted. Three days later a cease-fire was proclaimed in Evian, where Algerian officials had been negotiating with the French government.

After lunch, Christopher showed me the outside of the house that I later occupied as ambassador, as well as the offices where I would later work. I had forgotten them both when I took up my appointment. Then this rapid preview came back to me. I do not know if I am imagining it, but I believe it may have occurred to me that I might one day live in the house. Perhaps Christopher made a joke about it or perhaps, seeing Algiers for the second time, I simply thought that it was not going to be the last.

My third visit was only for a night in the autumn of 1977 shortly before I arrived as ambassador. My predecessor John Robinson, suggested that a preliminary inspection would be helpful to me from a housekeeping point of view — and indeed it was. He and his wife gave me much good advice, though I was better disposed to the Algerian government than he had become. I had been at school with John (was a year older than he was) and had greatly respected hi work on European integration. But I thought that his views on the Algerian government, and on the role of our embassy, had become too rigid. With its oil and gas reserves Algeria was, at least potentially, a country worth bothering about. There seemed to me no reason why, within prudent limits, we should not try to develop our interests there, however difficult and dictatorial the regime. I had already lunched with Lakhdar Brahimi, the Algerian ambassador in London, who had appealed for Britain to adopt a more understanding attitude. He said to me that he had always thought that the job of an ambassador was to bridge differences, not to enlarge them. I have always made this assumption, too. Of course, there are times when confrontation cannot be shirked; but, except in conditions of actual or impending war, diplomats ought usually to err in putting a better, not a worse, construction on their host government's actions.

John Robinson was an able, but obstinate man, who had trenchant views, which he expressed trenchantly. He had enjoyed his time in Algeria personally — he explored the desert at weekends and cultivated his kitchen garden in the evenings. But, he had no sympathy with the regime and, rightly or wrongly, took a bleak view of Algeria's prospects. As a result — rather unusually for a head of mission — he had cut his small staff quite substantially. When I took over, I had no head of Chancery, no defence attaché, no political officer and no archivist. The counsellor, Brian Hitch, was my deputy, leading the commercial section, which included a second secretary. There was an administrative officer/vice-consul and an accountant. I had my personal assistant. The rest of the staff was locally engaged. When I left Algiers this was still largely the position; I had only asked for, and got, the restoration of the archivist post. (My successor went on to recover a head of Chancery.) Throughout my time there, besides being ambassador, I did the sort of work I had done everywhere else at every stage of my career, down to weeding files. Because our contacts had become so few, this was manageable — it is only what ambassadors from smaller countries often have to do. But there was no slack and it did not help us to break new ground.

Although there was no need for me to supervise the ordinary business of the commercial section, of course there was some commercial work (for instance, calls on ministers) that only the ambassador could undertake. Because of Algeria's quite substantial oil and gas reserves, European and other countries were competing actively as suppliers of machinery and other manufactured goods. Among the European Community embassies, the Belgians seemed to be being particularly successful. I thought that British firms ought to be able to improve their share, however difficult and frustrating the market. This was the most obvious reason for trying to improve Anglo–Algerian relations. Whether or not because there was such an improvement, we did manage to increase our export figures during my time in Algeria, though — because of the subsequent fall in oil prices — they dropped again later. Perhaps the other main reason for getting on better terms was that, at that time, Algeria enjoyed a lot of prestige in the Third World, reflected in a surprisingly large diplomatic corps at the capital. This was at least partly due to the reputation that the Algerian foreign service had built up for activity and intelligence.

A third reason for seeking better relations was to minimize the risk of bilateral difficulties. British contacts with Algeria were minimal, compared with French. But they did exist. British Gas had regular dealings with the state-owned gas industry; British nationals worked in the desert. A few large British firms were interested in the country; one or two, like W. S. Atkins, were well established there. There were many Algerian students in Britain, while the British Council ran popular English courses in Algiers. The permanent British colony was small; but there was an Anglican church. Representatives of the British media, although not resident, did visit the country from time to time. It was worth taking such steps as we could to prevent friction.

There was no doubt that the Algerian government, at least when I took up my post, was thoroughly dictatorial. Boumédienne, the president, though not personally bloodthirsty, was tough and tyrannical; he and his colleague would not have taken any prizes as champions of human rights. They would have argued that Algeria had to be governed toughly, if it was not to fall into anarchy; they may well have been right. Their doctrine was that oil and gas profits should be used to make Algeria a self-reliant and industrialized power, not dependent — like its neighbours — on the patronage of foreign tourists. In practice, the oil and gas reserves had indeed been developed, but the profits had not always been wisely spent. We assumed that there was corruption in some places — though exactly how widespread and how damaging it was, no diplomat could hope to assess. On the social side, there was overpopulation, very inadequate housing and serious unemployment; at the same time, so far as one could judge, medical and educational facilities for the mass of the people had improved since the time of the French. Altogether, my personal reaction was to feel sympathy for the Algerian leaders rather than to condemn their mistakes. Even if this had not been my reaction, I would still have tried to improve relations, both for the reasons given above and because excessive Western criticism was more likely to make things worse than better.

The Algiers that I saw in 1977 was not the gleaming, sophisticated, place that had impressed me in 1956. In the main, it was shabby and dirty, though there were some new buildings and some picturesque remains. As a very rough generalization, I suppose one might say that the crowds in the streets looked dissatisfied, but not miserably depressed. The Algerians have always been regarded as a dourer people than, for instance, the Egyptians; they smiled less, though they could, and did, smile sometimes. Dour or not, they are intelligent and have staying power. They deserve better than they have had.

It was no easier in 1977 than it had been in 1956 to find out what was going on — harder, because in 1956 some Frenchmen had been ready to talk quite frankly. I have never been in a country where an atmosphere of secrecy seemed so endemic. Often, people did not have the answers. If they did have them, they were afraid to give them to foreigners. Partly this habit was ingrained, the result of centuries of foreign domination and piratical enterprise. Partly it reflected the Soviet system that the newly independent country had in some ways taken as a model. I knew that, in the early optimistic days of independence, Christopher and Jane Ewart-Biggs had been able to make personal friends of the Algerian leaders. By my time, the shutters had gone down. Ministers seldom paid social visits to foreign missions; we were never invited into their houses and hardly ever into the houses of other Algerians. There was a certain amount of official entertaining — large government dinners in honour of important visitors. That was all. Many heads of mission contented themselves with inviting each other.

One or two people told me that there was no absolute ban on Algerians accepting diplomatic invitations. So I made an effort, with mixed success. They would come when there was some good reason for it and their enemies could not accuse them of laying themselves open to foreign influences. Some felt secure enough to come on ordinary, as well as on special, occasions. Others were frightened by the prospect of meeting foreign businessmen. On the whole, if enough trouble had been taken, the results were not too bad. But there was no reciprocity. This was not surprising, given that few or no Algerians, other than ministers, had anything like ambassadorial facilities. Coming to my house they would say, more wistfully than resentfully, that I was showing them a side of Algiers that they had not known to exist.

Although the embassy offices were not particularly impressive, the residence was a handsome late nineteenth-century building that had originally been a British club. When it was built there was quite a substantial British colony in Algiers, consisting of people with money who had come there for the climate, often for convalescence. It was not as smart as Cannes, but offered some of the same attractions. There was a visit to Algiers by a Soviet warship during my time there. The diplomatic corps being invited on board *en masse*, I was in the queue just ahead of the East German ambassador and his wife, who was a scholar and an authority on Marx. She told me that 100 years before, to the day, Marx had visited a tsarist warship in the harbour of Algiers, where he was convalescing at the expense of his friend Engels. This struck me as a remarkable coincidence, both in itself and in its historical implications; she obviously thought so, too.

As well as a handsome house, I had a fine garden with views over the Mediterranean, a swimming pool and a tennis court. Sometimes, I shared the lawns with tortoises and the pool with exhausted migrating birds. Being a bit of a convalescent myself because of my kidney trouble, I preferred gentle exercise and became something of a bird-watcher. On one May afternoon, I counted 15 different species in the embassy grounds. The garden included several orange and lemon trees and some useful shrubs: a persimmon, a pomegranate and a verbena bush, with leaves that made soothing tisanes. Having taken over the Robinsons' Algerian servants, I had the same sort of establishment as I had had at Cairo, except for more garden staff. I also had a

chauffeur, who drove my official Jaguar. Its colour wa
British racing green and it excited the envy of my diplomati
colleagues.

Algeria is a very beautiful country. The greater, but leas
populated, part of it is desert. I did not explore much o
that, or see the famous Tassili cave paintings in the deep
south. To the north of the desert are steppes covered with
scrub, then a spectacular mountain range, then a fertil
coastal strip. Some of the towns are attractive or interesting
– Constantine, with its marvellous site, Bejaia (Bougie)
with a tranquil kind of charm, Gardaia, associated with Le
Corbusier, Tlemcen, with its Islamic architecture. There are
superb Roman remains at Timgad, Djemila and Tipasa.
visited most of the country north of the desert, at one time
or another, but I was a much less energetic traveller than
John Robinson had been. I mentioned his love of travelling
when I presented my credentials to Boumédienne, and
noticed a significant exchange of glances between him and
Bouteflika, the foreign minister. It occurred to me that they
had suspected him of spying – though of what, God knows.

I put as much goodwill as I felt I realistically could into my
initial calls. In London, I had found that the geographical
department concerned with Algeria had developed a hostile
way of thinking about the country, presumably under the
influence of my predecessor's reports. One or two senior
officials were uneasy about this, but there were other countries of more obvious importance to Britain for them to
worry about. It was a consolation to me in Algiers, to think
that the shift towards friendlier relations that I hoped to,
and I think did, bring about would have been less easily
attainable in places having wider British connections and
more publicity in the British press. At least as far as the
public was concerned, I had fewer prejudices to overcome. I
had some luck, too. Frank Judd, then minister of state at the
FCO, paid an official visit to Algiers not long after my

rrival. I did not need to persuade him to take a sympathetic
iew, or to be careful not to display the least sign of superi-
rity; he got on extremely well with his Algerian hosts.
3oumédienne received him personally and, at the end of the
nterview, told him that a British national, languishing in an
Algerian prison, would be released. The man had been
onvicted of drug smuggling under retrospective legislation,
nd this had become a bone of contention between the two
governments. I had hoped that the problem would be easier
o solve by soft words — and so it turned out. Later on, we
ecured the release of two or three other British prisoners.

At the end of 1978, Boumédienne died in his bed, partly or
mainly because of kidney disease. I was visiting Tlemcen, in
he west of the country, when he fell ill. In my absence,
3outeflika telephoned Brian Hitch and implored his help in
ecuring the services of a British specialist; this was
irranged, but Boumédienne was beyond medical help. After
iis death, there were meetings of the ruling party (the Front
le Libération Nationale); as usual, it was impossible to
ibtain reliable information about them. It was not till
'ebruary 1979, that the less autocratic Benjedid Chadli
issumed power. There was then a gradual, but general,
asing in relations with the West. One small sign of this was
hat the soldier who occupied a little lodge at the entrance to
ny grounds was withdrawn. (I suspected that his duty had
)een to keep an eye on, as much as to protect, me.) I did not
niss him; except for one occasion when he asked me for a
glass of water, we had only exchanged good mornings. But I
elt freer than ever to walk into the centre of Algiers on
Saturday evenings and have a meal at one Indo-Chinese
estaurant that had survived. I saw on television recently
hat the embassy now has to be guarded by armed soldiers,
ir policemen, stationed on its roof. I suppose that my suc-
essor is not allowed to walk anywhere on his own.

I think it must have been after the change of president that

the Algerian government arranged a wild boar hunt for th
diplomatic corps. It was well — and of course ver
hospitably — organized. We were put up for the night in
local hotel; after the hunt, we enjoyed a splendid feast in
specially erected tent. Sadly, the boars had taken note of th
preparations. One undersized animal was shot by an Algeria
and paraded round the feast; none of the rest of us encoun
tered any wild life at all.

I had a shotgun then, but I had left it in England. How
ever, my French colleague, who could not go, pressed me t
borrow a powerful sporting rifle. He warned me that i
would go off at the slightest touch, if the safety catch wer
released. I believed him, but did not realize how slight th
slightest touch could be. After the hunt, the frustrated head
of mission were unable to resist firing a few shots at a
improvised target. In between shots, I neglected to close th
safety catch and my rifle went off, seemingly of its ow
volition. Luckily, I was holding it correctly, so that it onl
struck the earth. I tried to look as impassive as I could; th
Algerian boys around us stared at me, in curiosity rathe
than alarm, as if I had just enforced a point made in conver
sation.

My Swiss colleague, who did not shoot, gave me a stif
dressing down afterwards and was only partly mollifie
when I explained that I really was quite used to shootin
(however badly), though not with such a highly-strun
weapon. This is one of the incidents in my life that stil
makes me sweat when I lie awake with indigestion.

Boumédienne had been in power over 13 years; the relativ
stability that his autocracy had achieved survived his death
at least so long as I was in Algeria. David Owen came ou
for his funeral, some weeks before Chadli emerged as hi
successor. We had expected Tony Benn, but there was an o
crisis and the Prime Minister thought he could not let hir
go. So the foreign secretary came instead. He was not bes

pleased, since it was his wedding anniversary and the funeral was not an occasion for serious political talks. However, the visit began well; he was intrigued to find an eighteenth-century coloured engraving over his bed that showed his Thames-side house. Next morning, I was able to take him for a drive around the capital. It was only after the ceremony, when the returning aircraft were held up at the airport by the pressure of traffic in France, that his patience snapped. He sent out his private secretary to me with a rude message to pass on to the Algerians. Of course, I did not convey it (I do not suppose he really meant me to); but I did manage to discover somebody who appeared to be directing operations and pretended that my job was at stake. When I got a promise that the aircraft would be released in ten minutes' time, I felt in a strong enough position to be rather rude in my turn to the foreign secretary. As I climbed into the aircraft, I found him reading one of Jan Morris's books about the British Empire. I told him that I had been on my feet for hours and I was as anxious for him to leave as he was. It was a relief when, exactly ten minutes later, the traffic controller kept his word.

In 1979, there was a change of government in Britain and the Conservatives were back in power. Early in 1980, Cecil Parkinson came out as trade minister and was as tactful with the Algerians as Frank Judd had been. In May, the Algerian foreign minister (who died in an aircraft accident a few years later) visited London for talks with Lord Carrington. During his visit, Mrs Thatcher received him in her room at the House of Commons. Mrs Thatcher seemed a little tired and, whether or not because of that, was very mild. She spoke about the crisis in Afghanistan, fearing that, if the Russians were allowed to get away with it, we could none of us sleep quietly in our beds. I doubted if it would keep the Algerian long awake; but, even if there was no real meeting of minds, he was as polite as she was. His real, perhaps his only, object in meeting the British prime minister was to be able to show to his colleagues that he counted for something internationally. I did not take part in the conversation; I felt that I was not expected to; besides, I had little to say. At the end, I thanked the Prime Minister profusely for giving up her time. She looked at me with what I took to be contempt. If so, I thought it was justified.

When I left Algiers, in May 1981, I was making arrangements for a return visit by Lord Carrington; my number two wrote to me afterwards that it had been a success. I was beginning to wonder whether we ought not to space out high-level visits more (we had also had one from the permanent undersecretary); but of course, it is difficult to ensure that visits are made at a time that is ideal for both sides. Certainly, they helped then to improve our political relations with Algeria and to lessen the distrust with which Algerian leaders tended to regard the West. They may have done our exports some good, too. Openings for more intensive economic cooperation were discussed from time to time but seldom came to anything. The Algerians were disappointed that, although an oil-producing country, we tended to approach oil problems as consumers rather than producers. When I first went to Algiers, much of our own enterprise was state-run; I used to take the line that we had a mixed, not a purely capitalist, economy. As this became less true, I suppose it was harder to establish a community of interest.

The highest-level visit of all took place in October 1980, when the Queen paid state visits in *Britannia* to the Holy See, Tunisia, Algeria and Morocco. The preparations were rather worrying because the palace expected a detailed programme some time in advance, while the Algerians specialized in brilliant improvisation at the last moment. Here, too, I had some luck. At the end of his visit in London, the Algerian foreign minister had said to me that they must rely on me to make sure that the programme for the state visit met the Queen's wishes. Armed with this rather vague authority, I drew up the programme myself, visited the places I thought she might be shown and timed the distances in my own car. When an advance guard from the palace came out to vet the arrangements, I took them to meet Algerian officials. There was a minor political crisis and we were kept waiting. I expressed indignation and disappointment in front of an embarrassed junior official. Not long afterwards, we were received and, amid the apologies, I was able to secure Algerian agreement to almost everything I had worked out. One of the highlights was to be a speech to the National Assembly; the Queen would have made it in French, but, as I had suspected, the Algerians preferred to have it in English.

Some days before the visit, there was a bad earthquake at El Asnam in the interior; I could feel the tremors at Algiers while I was lunching on my veranda. I had some advice — not from Algerians — that it would be better to postpone the visit. I thought that would be a mistake, but arranged for the Queen to visit victims in a hospital and for the Duke of Edinburgh to go to El Asnam. (I happened to be calling on an Algerian minister and was able to satisfy myself from his personal reaction that his colleagues would be disappointed by postponement.)

A second piece of luck was the timing of the visit. The royal yacht came alongside at Algiers on a Saturday morning. It was convenient for the British journalists covering the tour to arrive by air on the Friday evening beforehand. This gave me a chance to have them to drinks in my house and to answer their questions about Algeria. Douglas Hurd, who was to be in attendance on the Queen, spent that night as my guest; so, they were able to meet him as well; I think these arrangements may have helped to procure a better press in Britain than we might otherwise have had.

Apart from a couple of minor mishaps, everything went surprisingly well. I was glad to have spent two nights on board *Britannia*, to have been 'dubbed' in a cabin and to have had two protein-rich breakfasts, in spite of the disapproval of the Queen's doctor. The only hospitality I was required to give myself was a garden party for British nationals. This was the occasion for both of the two mishaps. The Algerian boyfriend of a member of the embassy staff was supposed to take photographs; he did take them but they did not come out. *Britannia*'s Royal Marine band was supposed to play on the lawn. I had hired a small bus to bring them to my house; they judged that it was too small and refused to come. On the whole, I was much less disappointed by what went wrong than relieved by what went right. I was particularly heartened by the crowds at the port (the Italian ambassador said that they were 'thirsty' for visual splendour), by the reception given to Her Majesty's speech and by the way in which she managed to converse happily in French with President Chadli throughout a long Algerian dinner.

The volumes of state papers on the bookshelves of my office contained a number of treaties concluded by our Stuart monarchs with the 'warlike' (piratical) city of Algiers. At my suggestion, fair copies of these treaties were presented to the Algerians, who complained of having no archives relating to the period before the French invasion of 1830. The Queen also referred to these treaties in her speech, in terms that led the *Le Monde* correspondent to report that we regarded them as still in force. The wording, which had been carefully chosen, did not in fact imply this; but no great harm was done if people thought that it did. Even after independence, we tried not to cross swords with the French over Algeria; but we could not let French susceptibilities entirely govern Anglo–Algerian relations.

Before independence, many right-wing Frenchmen sus-

ected the British of intriguing against their presence in
lgeria. Discussing Algeria in France was almost as tricky as
rguing about Israel in the Arab world. By 1963, all foreign-
eld agricultural land in Algeria had been expropriated and
y 1965 more than 80 per cent of the French population
ad left. But, of course, the French continued to have
nportant interests in the country and there was still a
iassive immigration of Algerians into France. The French
mbassy in Algiers had had to accept that their European
artners would do business with the Algerians without
sking their leave; as a rule, the French ambassador would
ike part amicably in the regular meetings of Community
eads of mission. But I think they expected their partners to
ecognize that their position was in some ways special; there
was occasional friction (for instance, during my time,
etween the French and Italian ambassadors). I do not
emember having any rows with the French myself, though I
are say that they did not like everything we did. The wide-
pread use of the French language, especially by educated
lgerians, was of course a commercial advantage for them
nd the Belgians. It was one of the things that hindered
ritish penetration of the Algerian market.

As in other ex-colonial countries, the Algerians had mixed
eelings towards their former rulers. There was sometimes
eal hatred. The war for independence had been fought
avagely on both sides; after a drink or two, Algerians
vould recall what they or their relations had suffered. But,
here was also liking for individuals and much respect for
'rench culture. My own impression was that the average
ducated Algerian had a deep inferiority complex towards
he French, as well as a lesser one towards other Europeans.
t seemed to me that the golden rule for any foreigner in
lgeria was to avoid stirring up this complex.

It would be hard to say whether I enjoyed my time in
lgeria. I found it an interesting as well as a beautiful

country; I was very well housed; Algerians treated me civilly
I liked being my own master. In a way it was the opposite c
Paris. There, my private life had for a time mattered more t
me than my work. In Algiers, I had virtually no private lif
except when I spent a free evening or weekend working o
the book I was now writing about Sir William Temple. M
social life and my travels were usually a part of my work; i
one way or another, I thought about it most of the time
This was to some extent a matter of age and seniority; I wa
happy to go into the office on Saturdays because it wa
nobody's business but my own whether I did so. It was als
because I had a serious, if controllable, disease. It is difficu
to explain, but my illness had somehow inculcated in me
sense of resignation. What with this and with the efforts
made to control my moods of impatience, I have never fe
more *moral* than in Algiers. I was schooling myself mor
than usual and trying harder to allow for other people's fee
ings. Perhaps I was not always successful; but I think I onl
once really lost my temper with an Algerian. All this was
morality based on my work. When I retired, and had n
work, I felt as if I had lost my morality, too.

I ought not to be too complacent about my behaviour i
Algiers. During my last weeks there, when the Foreig
Office did not seem to know what to do with me, I becam
rebellious. I did not always hide a sense of grievance fror
British visitors, though I hope I did from foreigners. I was i
this mood when the assistant governor of the Bank c
England came out to help broker the deal that procured th
release of the American hostages in Iran. I was not involve
in the negotiations. I did what I thought was required of me
but I might have done it more graciously.

I have never been back to Algiers since I left it 17 year
ago. I know no more of what has been happening there tha
the little I have read or heard in the British media. Before
left, there were already signs of a kind of Islamic revival. W

had tended to ascribe anti-Western feeling to communist or Marxist influence; it took time to realize that illiberal religious orthodoxy could prove as, or more, hostile. As in other Arab countries, Islamic fundamentalism was not only a reaction against imperialism and the West, but also an assertion of beliefs that owed nothing to any part of Europe. To some extent, such a revival became inevitable once the Soviet system broke down in Russia and could no longer be exported. God knows, there were enough unemployed and badly housed people in Algeria with grounds for dissatisfaction.

It was not inevitable that the revival should have taken the form that it has. At the outset, there was a clash between the more or less socialist values held by some Algerians and the traditional religious values held by others. Later, the conflict seems to have degenerated into a kind of gang warfare. Brutality and secrecy may have been endemic in Algerian society for centuries; they certainly marked the war for independence. But I never foresaw such prolonged and apparently senseless killings. I have not found them any easier to understand than other people do. It is only a partial explanation that, in some situations, violent men gain control and, under whatever pretext, satisfy their violent inclinations.

I do not know what view the Foreign Office now takes of Algeria and its future. Perhaps John Robinson was right, after all, when he judged Algeria to be a country with poor prospects, offering very limited scope for British enterprise. But, it is just possible that a corner has been turned and that things will begin, very gradually, to improve. Even if John was right, it would not follow that we were wrong in trying to bring about better relations two decades ago. The Queen's commission, when I was appointed ambassador, empowered me to promote 'relationships of friendship, good understanding and harmonious intercourse' with Algeria. Where there is any intercourse (and there was bound to be some), it had better be harmonious than otherwise.

10
Retrospect

On leaving Algiers, I would normally have had one other ambassadorial post before retiring at, or no long before, the age of 60. I thought I was well enough, physically, to cope with another three years. My doctor might not have agreed; but he was not asked to give an opinion. Whether I was fit enough, or not, there seemed to be no suitable post available. The Hague having been filled by another candidate, there was certainly no opening for any special qualifications that I had. So I took advantage of a scheme for early retirement.

I was sorry about this — and perhaps sorrier for myself than I should have been. But my sort of kidney disease though not painful, was debilitating; so I had some excuse for feeling depressed. As a younger man, I had often looked forward to retirement; when I actually experienced it, I longed for regular work. I missed coming home, tired, after a day in the office; when I woke up in the morning it was with a feeling of emptiness, not of release. I did not miss the trappings of being an ambassador; but my work had so much taken over my life that, once it was no longer there, I scarcely knew what there was of me left.

I had often thought that, in retirement, I would be able to write the books that I really wanted to write, with plenty of uninterrupted time in which to do so. It was partly with this in mind that I had started to write books, on historical topics, while I was still in the service. I began the first during

ny years in Paris; I had three others published before my
)osting to Algiers. The fourth, *French and English*, came out
vhen I was head of planning and attracted the most notice. I
inished my next book, on Sir William Temple, soon after
etirement; but it attracted the least. After that, I brought
)ut two further books. Although they were as much and as
vell reviewed as my earlier books had been, they sold fewer
:opies.

Gradually, I realized that publishers and booksellers were
10 longer interested in books likely to sell steadily, but
modestly, over a number of years, particularly if they fell
nto the dreaded category of 'mid-list titles'.

I had to write my first four books during my leaves, or
)ver long (Easter or Whitsun) weekends. I deliberately chose
iubjects that would not require research into abstruse pub-
ications or original documents. For instance, my third book
'*Proper Stations*) was about class distinctions in the Vic-
orian novel. It was easy, even pleasurable, to skim through
Victorian novels, on the lookout for relevant passages,
whenever I had a free evening. This did involve giving up
)ther indoor hobbies; but that would probably have happened anyway as I got older.

After retirement, of course, I had more time for research. I
:ould also do the actual writing at one stretch. When I
wrote my sixth book, about the ways in which the peoples
of the United Kingdom have interacted, I felt myself getting
into an intellectual and stylistic rhythm more compelling
than I had previously experienced. This was exciting, perhaps misleadingly so; but, at least it was therapeutic. The
gloom surrounding me since my retirement began to dissi-
pate and I recovered some of my sense of proportion. That
was in 1983. Five years later, I had a further stroke of luck.
After a short spell of dialysis I had a successful kidney
transplant.

I have sometime wondered whether I took the right deci-

sion in Athens on that summer evening half a century ago
On the whole, I think I did, in spite of the disappointment a
the end. I enjoyed a series of interesting and varied posts.
do not know what other career could have provided such a
range of experiences and impressions. I had some of the
qualities needed for my job, though not others. Diplomat
are supposed to be calm, self-effacing and patient —
cannot say that I always was, but I tried to control my
weaknesses. When I joined the service I expected, because of
a good academic record, to be better at handling paper in
London than people abroad. As it turned out, I believe the
reverse was the case. I was no better at deskwork than mos
of my colleagues, and worse than some of them. But I fel
that I developed a better insight than many into the way
foreigners thought and behaved. My basic fault — a
tendency to oscillate between diffidence and overconfidence
— will probably be clear enough from this book. It would
have afflicted me in any walk of life.

Perhaps because my parents had money, but not too much
of it, being rich never mattered very much to me. In thi
respect, I suppose I was more influenced by my abstemious
mother than by my expansive father. In any case, when I
joined the Foreign Service, most people from my sort of
background had been brought up to value professional
achievement and distinction above wealth. Of course, I was
lucky to be able to assume that I would always be adequately paid. I never managed to save any money as a diplomat. But I was able to live comfortably, sometimes very
comfortably, and I never fell into debt. What private money
I had was spent on maintaining a flat in England while I was
abroad.

I did not buy a really long lease on a London flat until I
was 42. Then, with the help of a legacy and a family loan, I
got a 60-year lease on a two-bedroomed flat in Ennismore
Gardens for £12,000; a few years later, when I was abroad,

sold it for a good profit. Subsequently, I found that I enjoyed doing up flats, living in them for a bit and then moving elsewhere. I have gone on in this way ever since, much to the despair of my friends' address books. More often than not, I have made a profit, though seldom as good a one as the first; but of course fees, expenses and inflation have quite often involved me in real loss. Yet, overall, I have wasted less money than might be supposed. I doubt if I would have acquired this hobby (for that is what it became) if I had not had to move so much inside the service. In three of my posts — Abidjan, Cairo and Algiers — I lived in houses furnished and owned by the British government. In the other posts I was given an allowance to rent accommodation. Since I moved twice in The Hague, and once in each of the other three posts, I occupied eight houses and four flats during my service abroad.

Before my retirement, I used to feel that it would have been easier, as well as more necessary, for me to save money if I had been married. I was certainly a good bargain for the taxpayer; I did not need any allowance for my wife's expenses; I had no children to be educated in boarding schools, and sent out for holidays abroad, at public expense. But, being unmarried was not a career asset; if anything, it may have held me back.

As far as official entertaining goes, I do not think being single was much of a handicap; it seemed to me that I entertained as actively as most married couples. Naturally, I needed a good enough cook; but so do senior diplomatic wives. There was no great difficulty in composing menus for parties. I found it more difficult composing lists of guests: this was a weekly, or fortnightly, chore throughout my career; but I would have had to do that anyway. If I had been appointed ambassador in a post that was busier socially than Algiers, I would have employed a housekeeper. Some embassies need to put up official guests more than others do. I could have supplied an adequate hotel service though I could never have made my house a welcoming social centre in the way that good hostesses do.

Although I could do the job without a wife, I would have done it better and more easily if I had been married to one whose heart was really in it. The trouble is that some wives are shy, or do not like living abroad, or — even in my time — wanted lives of their own. It can be amusing to be a young diplomatic wife entertaining for the first time. It can be rewarding to be an ambassador's wife running a big house in an exciting capital city. But, in between, there can be tracts of boredom and frustration. Single diplomats make better entertainers than wives who are absent, or indifferent, or resentful.

At a deeper, more private, level I often felt the need of a counsellor when I was abroad, particularly in the closing months of my time in Algiers. A wife, too, would have helped to form and maintain friendships that I had to neglect. But, having said all this, I was better as I was, than if I had been unhappily married.

I have dwelt a bit on my single state because people have sometimes asked me how I was able to manage. Like all diplomats, whether married or unmarried, I found that I had chosen a profession that offers great advantages, as well as great disadvantages. Perhaps, the former are the more immediately obvious. In my experience, the main attractions were the interest of the work, its variety, its standard of living and its privileged opportunities of seeing the world. Above all, perhaps, was the recurring fascination of getting to know a foreign country and its people.

The disadvantages were equally great, some might say greater. It was impossible to put down roots anywhere; one became a perpetual peregrine, even in one's own country. It was extremely difficult to maintain friendships at home. The discipline of the profession — the constant need for tact and discretion — had an inhibiting, as well as a polishing, effect. Social life was so much a part of the job that one began to feel disgusted with it. My father, a publisher, complained that his work had spoiled his taste for reading; I came to feel the same way about parties. Perhaps it is because of this suppressed disgust that diplomatic society, as such, though full of intelligent and agreeable people, can be so supremely dull; if I enjoyed diplomatic parties it was as work, not as relaxation. Then again, there are relatively few capitals with so much to offer as London. Some places have the charm of the exotic; others do not even have that. I had to get out of the habit of going to the theatre, because there was not any; I have never really got into it again.

Even the interest of the work, though considerable, is not constant. When nothing much is happening it can give way to boredom; when too much is happening it can tighten into anxiety. Sometimes, I felt absurdly that, unless I suffered from enough anxiety, the problem I was handling would not be successfully solved. I dare say that most serious work produces such tensions. Yet, few practitioners in other professions have to operate under such a load of superiors, official, ministerial, political and public. There are also few jobs where real success and failure are so difficult to judge. There are no profits to go up and down. More often than not, any successes are hidden. When they are apparent, they can turn into failures in the longer term.

Young people nowadays are being warned to prepare themselves for a series of jobs, not for a single career. From that point of view, diplomatic life is less old-fashioned than might be supposed. In effect, I changed my job every three years or so. In each post there were different problems to face, different people to know, different places to visit, different customs to learn. But, of course, there was continuity as well: continuity of structure, continuity of working methods and (at least in my case) continuity of themes.

Three main themes dominated the greater part of my career, each of them arising from the disbandment of our empire. First, there was the development of a new relationship with the Arab world; second, an orderly withdrawal from our responsibilities in black Africa; third, the forging of closer links with the countries of western Europe. These themes still thread the tapestry of our foreign policy. We have not yet fully determined our role in Europe; the past continues to haunt our relations with the Arabs; in parts of black Africa we have shed responsibilities only to find ourselves still involved, if more distantly and less exclusively. But our options, in all these areas, are not what they were when I was working. The biggest change of all has been the most obvious. When I was in the Northern Department I might have hoped, but I would never have dared predict, that the cold war would be over in my lifetime.

A candid friend once asked me, in a moment of irritation, whom I thought I represented when I went abroad. Her implication was that I was hopelessly untypical of my fellow countrymen. That may be true; I am not mad about football, I seldom drink tea and I have not had a pet since the white puppy in Baghdad. But, to represent people, one does not have to embody them. More seriously, how can any one person represent a country like Britain, with its vast range of classes, occupations, views and temperaments, by being typical of it as a whole? Even to represent the majority, he would have to assert a claim to be exceptionally 'ordinary' (whatever that may mean). I do not myself accept that the majority of the British people are 'ordinary'; I am certain that ambassadors should not be.

Ambassadors may have lost some of the glamour of their predecessors in earlier centuries, though hotels and laundries still find it profitable to use the title. But that is not because they have lost in importance relative to their staffs. Heads of mission still rule their own roosts; even the less commanding set the tone. Nor is it because they have less power and responsibility than they used to have; they have always had to operate within the limits set down by their instructions from home. Of course, in the seventeenth and eighteenth centuries, when communications were so much slower, they sometimes had to do things that had not been explicitly approved by central government. But the improvement in communications has cut both ways; it is much easier now for ambassadors to advise their governments on what their instructions should be. If there has been some devaluation in ambassadorial status, the main explanation is a simple one: there are so many more ambassadors than there were. In the heyday of British power we only had ambassadors in a few European courts. Since the war, there has been a dramatic increase in the number of independent countries as well as a raising of the level of diplomatic representation.

Diplomats, including ambassadors, ought to be judged as professionals. You employ the best you can find and afford, as you do in medicine and the law. It is true that, unlike doctors and lawyers, they do not need a long period of training, or a mass of specialized knowledge, before they get to work. There is no real mystique about what they do; it is mostly a matter of common sense. They try to influence foreigners by appealing to their interest, to shared ideals or to friendship; or, more aggressively, they try to put pressure on them, in one way or another. We have to use all these methods of persuasion in business, or in private life.

At the same time, the best diplomats must develop above average acumen and powers of persuasion, as well as the sense of proportion that comes with experience. They also need to be exceptionally articulate, both in speech and in writing. These are professional qualities that do not come automatically, but have to be cultivated.

Other, more moral, qualities are also necessary — though

perhaps these depend on character rather than on experience. Morality has not always been associated with diplomacy. Sir Henry Wotton, ambassador at Venice under James I, wrote a famous sentence in a German visiting book. He pretended to have written, ambiguously: 'An ambassador is an honest man, sent to lie abroad for the good of his country.' But, what he actually wrote was in Latin and only bore one construction: 'An ambassador is a good man sent abroad to tell lies for the sake of the state.' Of course this was a joke. Unluckily, it was read by a hostile Roman Catholic eight years later and used to discredit him and his master. Wotton had to pen an elegant apology to win back the king's favour.

Diplomats do not, as a rule, lie; they will go to great lengths to avoid lying. They know that frankness is the best way of attracting confidence and that they depend on their hearers believing what they say. But they do have to be 'economical with the truth' from time to time; they are not paid out of public funds to reveal secrets or to emphasize what is wrong in their home countries. I hope I have told no lies in this book. Whether I have always told the whole truth may be another matter.

* * *

At the outset I said that this would be a personal memoir, not a small piece of diplomatic history. What little it contains about the organization of the Diplomatic Service, or about foreign policy, is meant to show what my own views and impressions were at the time — rather than to convey any final judgements. When I was in the service I tried to form opinions on the main events of the day, even when I was not directly involved. In retirement, though I cannot help forming opinions sometimes, I do not have to pontificate on every problem. Perhaps I can be forgiven for pontificating a little on European politics in my chapter on The Hague. This is still such a live question that it is difficult to separate my views now from what they were then.

My opinions did change in the course of my career, but not to any very great extent. What changed were the circumstances in which I had to apply them. I do not think I began with many illusions that I later shed. I regarded diplomacy as an honourable and worthwhile profession at the end as at the beginning; I continued to believe in the efficiency of the service. From time to time, comment in the British press suggests that not everybody shares this belief, despite a rather exaggerated respect for the 'Rolls-Royce' brains of our diplomats. It would be odd if the service *were* incompetent, since it has always been able to attract recruits of high quality and to select them by quite a searching process of tests. In my experience, the degree of its competence was well recognized by foreign diplomats, few of whom could claim to have been so well briefed for contacts and negotiations. It certainly helped us to 'punch above our weight' and to prevent an erosion in power from becoming a landfall.

Of course, there were always criticisms that could be made. Officials were sometimes efficient without being imaginative, even when flying high. There had to be a 'departmental view'; but sometimes it was too rigid and took too long to change. I felt this more as I got older. As a young man, I was less worried by the way in which even the most sensible people tend to go with the herd. I thought that merit and good judgement were easy to recognize and would automatically make their way in the world, sooner or later. I did not realize that presentation often counts for more than content. But these were illusions about life in general, as much as about the particular profession I had joined.

I did sometimes wonder whether enough attention was paid in Diplomatic Service training, and in reports on personnel, to the importance of understanding the psychology of foreign peoples. We are an insular, and used to be an imperial, nation. There is a British tendency to suppose that, when foreigners behave differently from us, they are departing from some established norm and should not be taken too seriously. No doubt, this is a universal, not an exclusively British, tendency; but sometimes it seems particularly strong in this country. Although no diplomat would think crudely in this way, he might not make as much effort as he should to put himself in foreigners' shoes. Presumably, some knowledge of, for example, Chinese characteristics is conveyed in the course of hard-language training. Otherwise, one is (or was) left to pick up what one could, on the spot.

In my thirties, I got into the habit of thinking that people complicated matters too much, that the simplest procedures were the best and that non-essential activity should be kept to a minimum. There were times when I could have wished that colleagues felt the same way. But, looking back, I doubt if there was any more tendency to create work in the Foreign Office than in other comparable organizations. Most of the activity was really unavoidable.

As to foreign policy, my views were always, in some respects conservative (with a small c). I was sceptical about the international enforcement of human rights; pending the establishment of some international authority. I thought that governments should leave it to independent countries to manage their internal affairs. I saw little scope for giving foreign policy an ethical content, except in the traditional senses of avoiding aggression and honouring commitments. I believed it was my duty to do what little I could to maintain the strength and prestige of the country in its overseas dealings. (A plumber complained to me recently that the 'Great' seemed to have gone out of Great Britain. I doubt if he would have shared many of my views; but I, too, wanted to keep Britain as Great as possible.)

In other respects, my attitude became more liberal (with a small l). I had begun as a semi-imperalist, though within more or less realistic limits. After Suez, I accepted the need to abandon imperialist pretensions; it followed that we had to respect the independence of former colonies and try to make friends with them. In this new world, I thought that Britain's main priority should be nearer to home and that we should work for closer European cooperation.

* * *

When the Foreign Office is criticized, it is often because it serves as a whipping boy for the rest of the world. Before we developed our present system of government, foreign affairs were the prerogative of the monarch and his advisers. James I, for instance, was quite clear that he knew more about foreign affairs than his subjects and that it was not their business to tell him how to conduct them. Through its control of taxation, Parliament gradually won more say over foreign policy until, in this century, the monarch's influence became marginal. But, eighteenth- and nineteenth-century aristocrats — at least those who took an interest in diplomacy — were, like our monarchs, brought up with some personal knowledge of foreign (principally European) attitudes.

No doubt, our monarchs and aristocrats made mistakes, sometimes grave mistakes. They were, however, aware that their decisions must be taken in the light of probable foreign reactions. It seems to me that, nowadays, 'public opinion' is too often invited to express itself on external matters without any real knowledge of what is going on in foreign countries or any real reflection on how we might be affected by it. Meanwhile, the media, instead of trying to correct our insularity, often prefer to pander to our prejudices. Whether jokingly or not, some of the tabloids refer to foreigners in deeply offensive ways. Much of the controversy on Europe has been carried on as if we were living in a vacuum. Yet, no country has less excuse than Britain for ignoring the reactions of our neighbours. We have almost always been involved in major European wars, whether we liked it or not. We have always been dependent on overseas trade.

Diplomats cannot expect to be very popular with their compatriots. They have to face both ways. They work for their own government and nation; yet they cannot do this properly in a foreign country unless they feel for that country a kind of loyalty too. If they are to bring about 'good understanding and harmonious intercourse' they must give the government to which they are accredited the impression that, up to a point, they are on its side. Of course, patriotic politicians and journalists are right to insist that, in protecting national interests, diplomats should sometimes be tough as well as tender. However, what matters is the result. Toughness alone will seldom get foreigners to behave as we would like. Without superior strength, it will never do so.

Journalists have a difficult job and are usually very good at it. It is no criticism of them to say that shortage of time, proprietorial prejudice, and intense competition for readers do not create the best atmosphere for wisdom and calm judgement. We are all of us, up to a point, good judges of our own interests; we are not such good judges of the interests or reactions of other people. Diplomacy is about dealing with other people (or peoples). If the main questions of foreign policy are to be decided by elections and referenda, then the voters must be given informed — and, so far as possible, disinterested — advice.

The professionals in the Diplomatic Service are as fallible as other groups of people. But they do meet foreigners and have to live with the effects of our prejudices abroad. Those who aim to form — or prefer to follow — public opinion should not undervalue their experience.

In 1681 Sir William Temple wrote in his memoirs (on his retirement at the age of 53):

> I know very well, the Arts of a Court are, to talk the present Language, to serve the present Turn, and to follow the present Humour of the Prince, whatever it is: Of all these I found myself so incapable that I could not talk a Language I did not mean, nor serve a Turn I did not like, nor follow any Man's Humour wholly against my own.

Modern democrats would applaud such sentiments, when expressed under a monarchy. They ought not to condemn them now that 'the Prince' is public opinion, or what passes for it. Independence of judgement in public servants, whether elected or appointed, is as necessary as it was when 'the Prince' was one person.

Index

215

Index

216

Index

Index

Index

Index